RESURRECTING
JESUS

ALSO BY ADYASHANTI

Emptiness Dancing

*The End of Your World: Uncensored Straight Talk
on the Nature of Enlightenment*

Falling into Grace: Insights on the End of Suffering

My Secret Is Silence: Poetry and Sayings of Adyashanti

True Meditation: Discover the Freedom of Pure Awareness

*The Way of Liberation: A Practical Guide
to Spiritual Enlightenment*

RESURRECTING

JESUS

Embodying
the Spirit of a
Revolutionary Mystic

ADYASHANTI

sounds true
BOULDER, COLORADO

Sounds True, Inc.
Boulder, CO 80306

Published 2014, 2016

Cover design by Jennifer Miles
Book design by Beth Skelley
Cover photo © PavleMarjanovic from Shutterstock.com

Printed in the United States of America

ISBN 978-1-62203-763-6

Library of Congress Cataloging-in-Publication Data
Adyashanti.
  Resurrecting Jesus : embodying the spirit of a revolutionary mystic / Adyashanti.
    pages cm.
  ISBN 978-1-62203-094-1
  1. Jesus Christ—Buddhist interpretations. I. Title.
  BT304.914.A38 2014
  232.9—dc23
                                    2013033333

Ebook ISBN: 978-1-62203-162-7

10 9 8 7 6 5 4 3 2

This book is dedicated to my grandfather, Harold Foster.
He was the first true Christian that I knew in this life and a rare
embodiment of Christ's unconditional love. His capacity to
affirm the very best in everyone he knew transformed many lives.
May you eternally rest in God's great love, grace, and mercy.

CONTENTS

FOREWORD

In my 2008 book *The Wisdom Jesus*, I speak quite a bit about what I call "recognition energy." It's a core thematic element running through all four gospels from start to finish. "Who do you say I am?" Jesus either implicitly or explicitly asks, and the field immediately divides between those who "get" him and those who don't. The recognition drama begins early, with the very first calling of his disciples around the Sea of Tiberias, and continues right up to the very last moments of Jesus's earthly life when he is strung up on a cross between two fellow political criminals. One of them instantly recognizes Jesus's divinity, and one remains defiantly blind.

Jesus scholars—and over the centuries there have been a lot of them, a whole lot of them—traditionally point out that the ones who "get" Jesus are inevitably the poor, the oppressed, those with little to lose. The people who are most likely to perceive him as a threat are inevitably the *entitled* ones: the Pharisees, priests and other representatives of the religious and political establishment, and the very wealthy. But this isn't simply a matter of economic status, as traditional biblical scholarship likes claim. It's more a matter of what contemporary spirituality would call *identification*. The ones who are heavily invested in their roles, their ideologies, or their self-importance—in other words, those who have an ego-stake in the outcome—are the ones who can't see. It's the people who are *nonidentified*—inwardly and outwardly free enough to be capable of true beginner's mind—who are able to see the spiritual wisdom and light gleaming out from behind the unconventional religious packaging.

I say this with a specific intention in mind because I have the pleasure and honor of introducing this second edition of Adyashanti's *Resurrecting Jesus*. What I have loved about this book from the start is that it's clearly another profound example of recognition energy at work, with all the inner authority and luminous insight that pours from such an encounter. Adya certainly didn't *need* to write a book about Jesus in order to cement his growing presence as a writer and teacher. He has already powerfully established himself as one of the most important nondual teachers of our times, with an uncanny ability to cut through psychological knots and go straight to the core of things. But in his signature way—with that same transparency, clarity, and fearlessness—Adya simply made space when Jesus appeared on his internal radar screen and allowed the encounter to unfold. Forget that Adya is "supposed" to be a Zen Buddhist. What really matters is the integrity of practice—and the unimpeded clarity of authentic nonidentification.

But what happens when a teacher of Adya's spiritual magnitude focuses his attention on Jesus in such a singular act of recognition? "By your light we see light," as the old Psalm verse has it. He is able to see Jesus at something approaching the level Jesus is himself operating at. He grasps what Jesus's disciples—and the vast majority of the heavy-footed ranks following in their footsteps—have missed all along: that Jesus is himself a nondual teacher, arguably the first nondual teacher ever seen in the West. This is why he went right over people's heads—and why his teaching was flattened right from the start.

A nondual master teaches from oneness: not as a spiritual attitude or a philosophy, but as the direct perception of a mind (or better yet, a mind-heart working in unison) that no longer needs to divide the perceptual field in order to make sense of things. It is a whole new operating system, running a powerful "no-separation" program: no separation between God and self, self and neighbor, subject and object, inside and outside. Though it can arise as a spontaneous gift ("instant enlightenment" as Adya describes in this book), nondual perception is more typically the fruit of long and patient work on self, gleaned on the threshing floors of humility, compassion, and surrender. The Gospel of Thomas describes it well:

> When you are able to make two become one, the inside
> like the outside and the outside like the inside, the
> higher like the lower, so that a man is no longer male
> and a woman female, but together they become a
> single whole ... then you will enter in. (logion 22)

Ironically, for all the theological ink spilled during twenty centuries in the various dogmatic arguments and castles of speculation constructed in Jesus's name, there has been very little capacity to meet the teaching at the same nondual level from which it originated or to get it from the *inside*. The very concept of nonduality itself, as far as Christian theology goes, can barely be said to exist.

This is what I most appreciate about *Resurrecting Jesus*. It is an insider's view, the perspective of a person whose own deep fidelity to the path of conscious transformation has allowed him to recognize this "mind of Christ" for what it truly is: not so much a cosmic singularity (as Christian apologists have been *way* too eager to proclaim) but the next level of human consciousness emerging into manifestation. Adyashanti's brilliant revisioning of Jesus's mission in terms of the stages (and yes, the predictable plateaus and pitfalls) in the journey to full enlightenment is both deeply human and deeply encouraging to those of us who indeed seek to "resurrect Jesus," not as an object of adoration but as a living master whose footsteps we would more closely follow. And amazingly, even after all the centuries of theological ink, Adya is still able to bring some genuinely new insight here, particularly where matters of practical transformation are concerned.

And yes, this book will reflect "beginner's mind" in other ways. Adya is not a biblical scholar, nor has he spent long years in Christian schools of religion mastering the complex jargon and precise formulations that would make him *au courant* in the eyes of academic Christology. He is an amateur in the authentic sense of the term, which means a *lover.* Those of us who have been trained as "professional" scholars, exegetes, critics, and commentators would be well advised to forgive him the odd scholarly *faux-pas;* remember, it's we professionals who are the Pharisees of our own age!

In our one small and interwoven world, the great spiritual messengers of *all* the sacred traditions are a universal human treasure, to be received and reverenced with the respect due an attained being, an exemplar of a higher level of human consciousness. It gives me great joy to see that in recent years some of the best books on Jesus have been written by those outside the Christian tradition, whose mature spiritual insight has allowed them to pierce through some of those intricate theological webs in which we have attempted to pin him down and package him exclusively for ourselves. I consider *Resurrecting Jesus* to be one of those "best books." Whatever you may bring with you to the encounter with it, be it overpreparation or old wounds, I would invite you merely to open your own beginner's mind and let yourself be carried on these strong new wings that Adya furnishes. I guarantee that you'll appreciate the view.

Cynthia Bourgeault

EDITOR'S PREFACE

The Jesus you're about to encounter in *Resurrecting Jesus* is a spiritual revolutionary, an example of awakened humanity in action, beyond the confines of any religion or theology. This Jesus is not rooted in time and history; he points us toward the timeless realm of spirit. But neither is he distant and transcendent; his story is an invitation to embody spirit in the present, in ourselves.

When I first encountered Adyashanti's teachings on Jesus, I was captivated by his unexpected insights on Jesus as enlightened *being*. His talks brought Jesus alive for me in a way I'd never experienced before. I discovered that Adya's explorations of the gospel story were an annual Christmas tradition, one he clearly enjoyed.

When it came time to brainstorm a new project with Adya, I suggested that we ask him to teach on Jesus. As it turned out, he was already preparing for a week-long retreat on Jesus' life and teachings and was enthusiastic about creating a book and audio program on the topic.

So in the spring of 2013, I traveled with Tami Simon, Sounds True's publisher, to California to record the material that became *Resurrecting Jesus: Embodying the Spirit of a Revolutionary Mystic*. We spent four days in a comfortable studio tucked deep in the woods above Santa Cruz, listening intently as Adya shined a light on the deeper meanings of the Jesus story.

As Adya spoke, I was struck again and again by what a fantastic *story* the Gospels tell—especially the Gospel of Mark, the text at the heart of *Resurrecting Jesus*. From the moment Jesus appears at the River Jordan to be baptized, the story moves swiftly and inexorably toward the crucifixion, passing through joy and triumph, sorrow and betrayal along the way. In the light of Adya's teaching, the Jesus that comes through is deeply human, fully divine, and completely unexpected.

Throughout these talks, Adya draws from two translations of the Bible, the New International Version (NIV) and the English Standard Version (ESV). For each quotation, he's chosen the version that works best in context; the source Bible is indicated along with the chapter and verse. The other key text here is the gnostic Gospel of Thomas, a Coptic-language collection of sayings attributed to Jesus.

Listening to Adya in the studio and, later, editing the manuscript of this book, I began to see the ways in which these teachings close the gap between us and Jesus, between us and the divine. Just as Adya's Jesus is a revolutionary figure, *Resurrecting Jesus* is a revolutionary book—one that challenges our conventional interpretations and confounds our expectations at every turn. The Jesus story as Adya shares it is a blueprint for the awakening process, a teaching that shows us how *we* might embody divine being in human form—just as Jesus did.

Yes, Adya teaches Jesus is the son of God—and in the same way, each of us is the son or daughter of God. Each of us is the word made flesh. So what does it mean to resurrect Jesus—to free him from the accretions of history, theology, and belief? What does it mean for the Jesus story to come alive in *you?* Find out! That's the invitation of *Resurrecting Jesus*.

Mitchell Clute
Editor & Producer, Sounds True
Boulder, Colorado
April 2014

PROLOGUE: JESUS THE SPIRITUAL REVOLUTIONARY

Jesus is the silent colossus that has defined Western culture for the better part of two thousand years. He's the central persona in Western culture's collective dream. In the last few decades, the scholarly emphasis has been on trying to figure out which parts of the Jesus story are historical and factual and which aren't—in other words, what really did happen in Judea two thousand years ago? The scholarly interest in Jesus has been what did Jesus *really* say as opposed to what he didn't say. My view is we'll never really know with any certainty; we can't really know what happened and what didn't happen, or how much is historically true and how much is mythological. This search for the historical Jesus, although it's interesting, even fascinating, ultimately misses the point. The point is the *story;* the point is the collective dream.

In Western culture, we have for the most part forgotten the power of story, the power of myth to carry and transmit truth—ultimate truth, spiritual truth. Myth is that which speaks to our souls. Myth is the language that connects with our unconscious and brings forth the sense of eternity, of radiance peering through the world of time and space. Myth, ultimately, is a way of talking about what can't be said, of conveying what can't be written about. And so the Jesus story, I believe, comes most fully alive when we can let go of the obsession with history, of what did or didn't happen.

In the end, it doesn't really matter whether we read the Bible as historically accurate and factual or whether we read the story as mythic and metaphorical, as that which can carry truths of the divine to our conscious and unconscious *being* and help reveal to us something that facts can't touch upon. There are many ways to look at this story and to look at the character of Jesus. Each of us, hopefully, looks at the story in our own way, in a way that speaks to us. In *Resurrecting Jesus,* I'm looking at the Jesus story through a particular lens. My interpretive lens focuses on bringing forth Jesus the spiritual revolutionary, Jesus as a presence of divine radiance and enlightenment that breaks the boundaries and lines of separation that confine us—whether those lines of separation are cultural, interpersonal, tribal, or simply within our own psychology.

For me, Jesus the revolutionary has a unique way of unpacking the radiance of spirit, and so in this book I want to offer that particular lens, that viewpoint. But in the end, each of us will interpret the Jesus story in the way that's most relevant to us; that is how it should be. In fact, that is how it *needs* to be, because if we only look at someone else's interpretation, if we only look at it through one lens, then it completely gets in the way of our innate and unique creativity. So while I'm going to look at the Jesus story through the lens of Jesus the revolutionary, the important thing ultimately is that we each enter this story in such a way that it comes alive for us.

Looking at the Jesus story through the lens of Jesus the spiritual revolutionary is a means of bringing the story fully alive. Looking through this lens, I feel, breathes life back into the story, so it comes alive in a way that's beautiful and simultaneously very challenging, because Jesus the spiritual revolutionary has the capacity to wake us up from our own individual dream of separation and isolation.

In Western culture most of us have come to see Jesus as the embodiment of the highest form of ethics and morals—he is the good shepherd, we are the flock, and he's showing us the way. This is the Jesus of the churches; the churches are very much drawn to Jesus the ethical and moral preacher. This makes sense, because the ethical and moral domain is part of what any religion sustains and brings forth and transmits into culture. But if that is *all* we see in the Jesus story, then it ultimately blinds us to the underlying transcendence, to the radiance of the presence of Jesus. Without that transcendent radiance, Jesus just becomes another figure in the long history of moral and ethical prophets.

We know that how the culture at large has defined and interpreted the Jesus story is no longer speaking to many people's hearts in a deep way. Attendance in churches is declining at an alarming rate. Last year I visited Europe and saw amazing cathedrals, some of them over a thousand years old. These cathedrals are the proof that there was a time when the Jesus story was vibrantly alive and informing society. But most of these churches are empty now, and that tells us something important. That tells us that the church as a whole has failed to reinterpret the story and the message to remain current and *vital,* as something that speaks to our hearts, that speaks to those mysterious impulses within us, that allows us to lean into the mystery of our *being.*

So I think we need to look at the story anew. When we begin to interpret the Jesus story mythologically, we begin to look for its metaphors and symbols. We begin to ask, "What do the metaphors mean for me? What does Jesus stand for in me?" If we don't view Jesus merely as a historical figure who was born, lived, walked on the earth, taught, brought forth his message, and then died on the cross, and if instead, we look at Jesus also as a timeless living presence, as a metaphor for eternity within us, we can begin to step into that place inside where we become the sons and daughters of God. Then the story is revitalized. Then the Jesus story can come to life in a way that's truly meaningful for us. Of course, for many people this may be quite challenging. For some, it may even seem blasphemous to really embody the story in the way that I'm suggesting. But I think that all of the invitations to do so are right there in the story itself. When I really listen to what the stories have to say, it's as if Jesus is saying, "Come, come into the Kingdom of Heaven. The Kingdom of Heaven exists on the face of the earth, and men and women do not understand it." It seems to me that the presence of Jesus is a living embodiment of eternity, an embodiment of what exists within our own selves.

The Jesus story is a mirror that helps us to see ourselves more clearly. The primary function of mythic storytelling is to render life transparent to the underlying transcendence that shines through it. This is the power of storytelling. Storytelling invites us into a creative relationship with the story. We can't just be onlookers at a distance; we must throw ourselves into the story so that we start to become the characters. We must allow ourselves to see life with the eyes of Jesus, with the eyes of Christ, to see the world through the eyes of the disciples, through the eyes of those who were healed and made whole and redeemed by the Christ presence.

As I said, each of us will have our unique way of looking at the Jesus story. What I want to bring forth is one particular view that I think is very powerful and potent and relevant for our time. But as we enter together into the story, I also want to invite you into your own creative relationship with the story itself. Keep your ears open to how each part of the story is speaking uniquely to you. When we listen in this way, this two thousand-year-old mythic journey of Jesus becomes our own journey into ourselves, into the revelation of God within us, into the realization of who and what we really and truly are.

Adyashanti
Los Gatos, California
April 2014

PART
ONE

ENCOUNTERING JESUS

MY CONNECTION
TO JESUS

I can nourish myself on nothing but truth.

ST. THERESE OF LISIEUX

So how does a spiritual teacher with a Zen Buddhist background get interested in the Jesus story? Well, from the time I can remember, I was fascinated with the Jesus story. As a kid I watched *The Ten Commandments* and all the other spiritual epics that were on TV and in the movies at that time.

When I was young we had sliding glass doors on our bathtub, and I'd sit in the bath and doodle crosses with circles around them in the steam on the glass. Any time I had a piece of paper I would doodle cross signs with big circles around them. I didn't even think about it as a Christian symbol, and I didn't consciously connect it to the Jesus story, but my notebooks from the time I was in grade school all the way through college are filled with crosses. When I look back on that, I think that the whole story of Jesus and the image and symbol of the cross was lodged in a deep place in my unconscious; there was something really deep within me that was profoundly interested in this character.

Now, I didn't grow up in a particularly religious family, and I wasn't really interested in organized religion. When I was young, maybe eight or nine, my parents decided to take us kids to church for a while. Of course, I was put into Sunday school and my parents went off to what I called the "Big Room," to listen to the preacher. After two or three Sunday school experiences, I told my parents I didn't want to go anymore. The Sunday school teacher had us coloring pictures of Jesus in a book and singing songs, and I was more interested in what was happening in the Big Room, where the preacher and all the adults were. After a few weeks, we stopped going and that was that.

While my family wasn't particularly religious in the conventional sense, there was a lot of religious and spiritual conversation that went on in the family among my parents and my grandparents. I had two sets of grandparents that lived very close to me, as well as aunts and uncles and cousins, and we would all get together quite often. It was not unusual for the conversation to turn to various religious and spiritual subjects. Both sets of grandparents were churchgoers, and one of my grandfathers was what I'd call a "real Christian"; he embodied the Christian spirit of generosity and love in a way that I have rarely seen since. His friends called him "the deacon," because he spent so much time serving as deacon in his church.

These conversations had a deep influence on me. I just found them so mysterious and so engaging, these talks about God and spirit and Jesus, and as a child I would just sit there and listen with a kind of awe. I didn't understand it all, but it engendered in me a deep feeling of the mystery of life, of a transcendent presence that I could sense. Fortunately, the discussion was always very open and expansive, not dogmatic. Nobody was trying to argue their point; it was more a kind of inquiry, of really looking deeply at these things.

From the time I was very young, I would have various types of what I'd now call spiritual experiences, and when I heard talk of religion or spirituality, I made a connection between those experiences and some of the subjects the adults were discussing. So, as I said, even though we weren't a religious family, religion and spirituality were a part of life from as far back as I can remember.

I was also always a lover of Christmas. Now, I suppose any kid is a lover of Christmas, with all the presents, the tree, the lights, and those holiday TV specials made for kids. I loved all that stuff too, but for me Christmas was also a sacred time. Each year starting in October, I would be overcome by a certain kind of *presence*—a transcendent, beautiful, rich, intimate presence. I associated it with the Jesus story, which is, of course, what Christmas is really all about.

This feeling of the sacred would overcome me for several months before Christmas. The closer I got to Christmas, the more this sense of the sacred would overtake me. It carried a sense of great meaning and profound intimacy. I was literally living in a state of grace for two or three months every year, and this added a sacred dimension to the whole Christmas celebration that went far beyond the packages and lights and glitter of Christmas. And so Christmas and the Christian message have always resonated with me on a deep level; the Jesus story has always been significant to me.

As I got older, sometime in my teens, I partook in communion at a Catholic mass. I didn't know that you weren't supposed to take communion if you weren't confirmed into the church. Looking back, I'm glad that I didn't know I wasn't supposed to be doing that, because I did it innocently, and as I went through the ritual of taking communion and drinking the wine, I found this silent ritual to be extraordinarily profound. I didn't expect it to happen; I had gone to mass with another family, and I participated just to see what it was like. It also served to connect me, again, with the Jesus story.

FALLING IN LOVE WITH ST. THERESE

As I got into my late teens, I really started to get interested in a deeper form of spirituality. I wasn't thinking of Christianity at the time. I'd started to read some spiritual books, and in a book about Zen Buddhism I came across the word *enlightenment.* When I read the word *enlightenment,* I had a huge response to it, one that really changed my life's orientation. I just *had* to know the meaning of that word. I suppose you could say that was the moment I became a spiritual seeker; I was searching for the enlightenment I had read about in that Zen book.

I found a Zen teacher in a directory, one who actually happened to be only fifteen minutes from where I grew up, which was amazing because at the time there were very few Zen centers or temples in the United States. Her name was Arvis Justi, and she had gone through training with her own teachers for a long time. She actually taught out of her house. I was about twenty years old when I found her, and I studied and meditated with her for more than a decade. Eventually, when I was thirty-three, she asked me to teach.

Zen training is really focused on what you *do*—in other words, how you engage in a real practice that can open you up to the deeper dimensions, the deeper realities of the mystery of all of us. And so I was engaging in Zen and doing a lot of meditation. Sitting in silence was the primary practice, and it was a profoundly meaningful experience for me; it was really the avenue through which I engaged my spiritual search.

But as the years went on, there was something in the practice of Zen that I couldn't find a connection with; it started to feel a bit dry. I didn't feel deeply engaged on an emotional level. And so, without being really conscious of what I was doing, but just following my interest and intuition, I started to reach out again, especially through my reading. One day I found myself in a tiny spiritual bookstore in Palo Alto, California, where I found the autobiography of St. Therese of Lisieux. St. Therese was a nineteenth-century Catholic nun who died very young; during the last years of her life, her Mother Superior asked her to write down her life's story. Thumbing through her autobiography in the store, something about her saintly piety just intrigued me, so I bought the book and took it home.

As I read her life story, I was so taken by her; there was an innocence and a dedication to God that really touched something in me. Her relationship with God was very sincere and very simple, and something about the simplicity and sincerity of her approach touched something that was very sincere and simple in me. And much to my surprise, I found myself quite literally falling in love with this saint, who was long dead. And when I say I fell in love with her, I mean I *really* fell in love, like when you get a crush in high school, and you're completely preoccupied with someone. I read three or four different versions of her autobiography, I read commentaries on her life and her writings, and I was completely swept up with her for about two years in this love affair of the heart. I was caught so off guard by this experience, and it was so unexpected that I didn't really know what to do with it.

What was really happening was that my heart was being opened. There was something in the way she conveyed her real *love* of God that was deeply heart-centered, and it broke my heart wide open. This was the beginning of discovering within myself what I think of as the transmission of Christianity and of the Jesus story, which is the transmission of the love of the sacred heart, of the deep, open, unguarded intimacy of love.

I continued my Zen Buddhist practice—seeing my teacher, doing my meditation—but with my heart blown wide open it was such a different experience than before. That love was the missing element, what I hadn't found in my Zen practice. And, of course, looking back, I see it *was* there; it just wasn't there in a way that I could connect with. That makes good sense, of course, because I didn't grow up in a Buddhist culture, so it wasn't easy for me to connect with their icons, images, and stories. They're a little alien to me. Zen for me was about engaging in spiritual practice as a serious in-depth investigation. But through the Jesus story and through St. Therese, I started to experience the heart of sacred love. She was the doorway through which I walked deeper into the truth at the core of Christianity.

"THIS IS HOW I LOVE YOU AND HOW YOU SHALL LOVE ALL THINGS"

Not long after my encounter with St. Therese, I had a profound experience while at a Zen retreat. Zen retreats are very strenuous, with as many as fifteen forty-minute periods of meditation each day, so it required *a lot* of silent sitting, a lot of being in quiet. I had been to Zen retreats before and had just begun to think I was getting good at it when I showed up at this seven-day retreat. I was really looking forward to being there, but as the retreat unfolded, something started to go haywire. It began to turn into a nightmare. I felt an intense sense of discomfort, and I had no idea why it was happening. I felt a feeling of profound confinement, like a caged animal, and I wanted to break out.

Now, by that time I knew how to sit in meditation through all sorts of different states of mind and emotions, and I had long since realized sometimes you just have to sit through these discomforts. But this really had me stumped; I was so profoundly emotionally uncomfortable, with intense anxiety and fight-or-flight symptoms going on inside me. At a certain point I literally couldn't take it any more. I just cracked. It was devastating for me; I felt humiliated in a very profound way. And so I wrote a little note to say that I was leaving, and when everybody else was meditating, I tacked it up onto the teacher's door. You weren't supposed to leave without seeing the teacher in person, but I was so humiliated that I just couldn't face him. I left the note and got in my car and drove home.

I was so devastated that I really thought that this was the end of my quest. I thought to myself: *Well, you gave it a good five or six years, you really put yourself all into it, but you failed. You're not cut out for this; throw in the towel.* I was twenty-five years old, and I was certain, absolutely certain, that that was the end of my spiritual search. So I drove home thinking it was all over, but when I pulled up at my house, a little voice in my head said, "Just go right through the front door and out the back, sit down in your meditation hut and meditate." I'd learned to trust that still small voice in my head over the years. It didn't make any sense to me because I was sure that this was the end of my spiritual search, that it was all over, but I just did what the voice said. I literally walked from the car, in the front door, straight through the house to the back door and into my meditation hut.

No sooner did I sit down than that spiritual heart—the heart of love I'd first experienced reading St. Therese—literally exploded. It wouldn't even be true to say it expanded; it was like an explosion in my chest. I went from a state of despondency, certain that my whole spiritual search was over and I had failed, to this immensity of love, of a well-being beyond anything I had ever experienced. And then I heard these words in my mind, as if the God of the Bible was talking, and the voice said, "This is how I love you, and this is how you shall love all beings and all things." It literally felt like the voice of God, and that explosion of the heart changed everything.

That night the teacher from the Zen temple called me up, and asked, "So, what happened?" I said, "I don't know!" He asked, "Why don't you come back?" and I said, "Ok, I'll be back tomorrow!" That was the end of the conversation; it was literally that fast, because I didn't have any reservations about going back. I didn't necessarily feel that my spiritual life was back on track, but in this immensity of love that I'd experienced, I felt like a feather in the wind. Come back? Ok, I'll go back.

So I drove back to the temple, and as I was about to enter the meditation hall, I saw the retreat leader, the one who holds people to the rules. At the door of the hall, this monk looked me straight in the eyes and said, "You shouldn't have left, and you shouldn't have come back." And, you know, those were the best words he ever could have said, because I saw that, when he spoke, nothing in me budged—that love didn't shrink, didn't diminish, didn't move one iota. In fact, I just wanted to throw my arms around him and kiss him, because he showed me that nothing could budge what I was experiencing.

If I hadn't had that open heart and someone had said, "You shouldn't have left, and you shouldn't have come back," I would have been devastated. Instead, the effect that it had was simply to show me the immensity and the intensity of the love I was experiencing. I walked right back in that door, and I had a wonderful retreat.

And so what began with this Christian saint opening my heart in a totally unexpected way, really culminated in this blasting open of the heart in a moment of great despair. Once again, the Jesus story—and this saint so intimately connected with the Jesus story—played a pivotal part in my life.

It was at this point that I began to read an immense amount on Christian mysticism—as many as two hundred books of the Christian mystics. I've told people since that I came to understand Zen through Christian mysticism, and in a way it's true. It was through Christianity that I really started to get a deeper understanding of what Zen was all about. Conversely, my Zen Buddhist practice and all my time in meditation helped me realize what the Christian mystics were saying, so they really went together for me at that time.

Through my reading, I also got a deeper feeling for the story of Jesus, both who he was and what the Jesus story meant to different people. In reading the mystics, I realized that the truth and the love of Christ meant different things for different people. Different mystics had very different takes on the relationship between Jesus and God, on their relationship with God and on their relationship with Jesus. I felt as if I'd walked into a mysterious world. As a child I was always intrigued with the Jesus story in a very powerful way; my imagination was captured by it. But when I stepped into the world of these ancient Christian mystics, I started to look at the story of Jesus in a completely different light. They showed me that the Jesus story could actually tell you something really important about yourself—how you relate to life and how you relate to the fundamental mystery of *being*.

For each of us, our own existence is a very mysterious thing. Simply to be, to exist, is a great mystery. On the surface, we each have a personality, a persona, an ego structure—the way we present ourselves to the world. But inside of us is something quite different. Now, in my twenties I'd gone to college and studied psychology and sociology, so initially I thought of what was inside in psychological terms. Then, through my study of Zen, I realized that there was a dimension of *being* that was far beyond what we would think of as our own personal psychology. Finally, when I encountered those Christian mystics, it's as if they pulled me into a more creative place, toward a meeting place where the story of Jesus came together with the creative power of the unconscious. That's a very powerful dynamic, when the mystery of our own *being* meets a really extraordinary story. That meeting can elicit something quite transformative.

THE CHRIST PRESENCE

And so here I was with this big open heart, studying the Christian mystics. I was taken not only with their words, but also with what my reading was waking up within me. A certain presence or vitality was awakened in me—a distinct and profound presence that belongs to the Christian tradition as a whole. In Europe, all you have to do is walk through the doors of those old churches and you immediately feel a distinct transmission, very different from the transmission of Buddhism or Hinduism or Islam or any other religion. Of course, each religion does have its own transmission, its own presence.

It comes from the founder of the religion, from their essence and from the hundreds or, in the case of Christianity, the thousands of years of different people relating to that core story. When we open to this Christ presence, it can evoke an inner sense of vitality and of boundless love.

As I delved deeper into these Christian mystics, I was beginning to question in my own mind if I needed to make a path change from Zen Buddhism to Christianity. It had been many years since I'd been to my first Catholic mass, and I decided to go back a second time. This time, I knew I wasn't supposed to partake of the communion, so when everyone else got up, I just sat in the back and watched. Even in watching, I found that there's a certain profound mystery about that ritual that is very hard to convey in words. Any powerful religious ritual will have this quality of touching something very deep and very ancient within us. A good ritual is meant to evoke the mystery of *being*, the mystery of our own existence, the mystery of life, the mystery of God. It's meant to evoke that sense of eternity that shines through the latticework of time and space. That's really what ritual is for—to put us in touch with that sense of eternity, with the sense of the sacred.

And so I was sitting in the back of the church and watching people go through the communion. Reading the mystics, who wrote so eloquently about their own profound experiences, I had felt a deep sense of connection, as if I'd reached back hundreds of years and connected with the living presence of another person. So I had an unconscious expectation that I was going to have the same feeling when I walked into this church and watched the mass. But when the priest started to talk, it was extraordinarily disappointing. He talked about abortion, about how families should be, about intimate issues having to do with sexuality and how you should live your life, and as he talked, I felt that he had taken the presence created by this ritual of communion and thrown it on the floor and stepped on it. I had a sense that he had *completely* missed the Christian message. He was more interested in modifying people's intimate behavior and in espousing certain political views, than he was with a priest's primary job, which is to open us to the mystery, to make the Jesus story transparent to the transcendent presence that it evokes.

As I listened to this priest, all the presence and mystery disappeared from the room and everything returned to the relative

13

world. That was the moment when I realized, "Ok, I guess the Christian path isn't going to be my chosen path." I wanted something really deep, and I could find it in the ancient mystics, but I couldn't find it in a living, modern church. But even though I knew that Christianity wasn't going to be my primary path, I also realized that the whole story of Jesus and the transmission of Christianity would continue to play an important part in my own spiritual development. My Zen meditation had gotten me to a certain point, but I needed the spiritual heart to flower so that I could keep going and not stall out. The Christian transmission has informed my whole spiritual path, and in a way it's informed my whole life.

THE JESUS
OF THE GOSPELS

> Jesus said, "I have cast fire upon the world,
> and see, I am guarding it until it blazes."
>
> GOSPEL OF THOMAS

ow let's fast-forward a dozen years. My Zen teacher had at this point asked me to teach, and I began sharing the dharma—giving talks, having retreats, following the trajectory of a contemporary spiritual teacher. I have never felt like it was my aim as a teacher to spread Buddhism, and in fact my teacher didn't even ask me to try to do that. What attracted me to spirituality at the very beginning—the question, "What is enlightenment?"—is what I'm primarily interested in as a teacher and what I'm there to awaken in the hearts and minds of the people who come to be with me.

In the course of my teaching, I discovered that whenever I talk about the Jesus story, it tends to resonate with people. That's not surprising, because the Western mind has been dominated by Christianity for more than two thousand years, so whether you're Jewish, Buddhist, Muslim, or even atheist, you can't help but be impacted by this story. This fact alone makes the story worthy of reexamining, and in doing so, we might find that the Jesus we've been told about is very different from the Jesus in the Gospels. That's what I hope to investigate.

READING THE GOOD NEWS

Like many people, my sense of who Jesus was was primarily informed by the prevailing culture. The Jesus that I knew was really the Jesus that I saw on TV and in movies, the Jesus depicted from the pulpit, and later the Jesus that I found when I studied the mystics, which was a mystical Jesus. These were the faces of Jesus that I had gotten to know through the first thirty-five years of my life. It may seem strange, but even through all of my study of the Christian mystics, I had never actually sat down and read the four Gospels. I never really read through the biblical story of Jesus. And when I did, I was amazed, even stunned, by what I found.

The Jesus that I found in the Gospels wasn't like the Jesus that I had absorbed through my culture or even the Jesus brought to life by the mystics. What I found in the story was an incredibly revolutionary figure, someone who broke down barriers and lines of separation, whether in the culture at large, in the political arena, or in the religion that he was brought up in. When I read the Gospels, something in me deeply connected with Jesus the revolutionary mystic, the one who is actually courageous enough to move through life guided and inspired by the dynamic of his spiritual essence. Seeing Jesus through the lens of the spiritual revolutionary is powerfully transformative; if we can embody that spirit within ourselves, we can begin to break down the internal walls that separate ourselves from each other, from the world, and from our own divinity.

There are many lenses through which to view the Jesus story. Jesus the revolutionary is, I believe, one of the most powerful lenses for our contemporary spiritual culture. Our contemporary culture and religion needs an influx of new life. I think the churches in this country need to be revitalized; they need that challenging presence of Jesus that says, "It's important that you realize the truth of your *being*. There are profound consequences to living in darkness." As Jesus says in the Gospel of Thomas, "If you do not bring forth what is within you, what you do not bring forth will destroy you." [Gospel of Thomas 70]

Jesus as revolutionary is a powerful lens, but as I said, it's not the only one. In each of the four Gospels of the New Testament, we get a unique portrayal of Jesus. Each one of the gospel writers looks at Jesus and his story through a unique interpretive lens. The Gospels of Mark, Matthew, Luke, and John each offer a different interpretation of the story. The gospel writers differ profoundly in where they put different elements of the story, with some gospel writers placing certain scenes at the beginning, others at the end. It's very clear that the writers of the Gospels were writing this story very creatively in order to create different meanings and convey differing agendas. Each offers a different portrait of Jesus.

THE GOSPEL OF MARK

I find that the lens through which the Gospel of Mark looks at Jesus is particularly compelling. In this gospel, Jesus is portrayed as a real revolutionary and also as someone who throughout the story is embodying a paradox: he has awakened to the reality of his own divinity, but he's still searching for his role in the greater culture and experimenting to see how to convey what he has experienced. I think that evolving role, that search for the complete revelation of what and who he truly is, is particularly relevant for our culture.

The Jesus portrayed in the Gospel of Mark has true spiritual autonomy; in the modern vernacular, you might say he is his own man. Now, many people have probably heard of egoic autonomy, of reaching a place in your inner psychology that is more coherent and not so conflicted, so that you can actually be a potent and vital presence in the world. But spiritual autonomy, as Jesus embodies it, goes *far* beyond that.

Spiritual autonomy is knowing who and what you are— knowing that you are divine *being* itself, knowing that the essence of you is divinity. You are moving in the world of time and space, appearing as a human being, but nonetheless you are eternal, divine *being*, the timeless breaking through and operating within the world of time. To Jesus, spirit is *everything*. Nothing matters more than spirit or, as I like to say, divine *being*. Divine *being* is what Jesus is here for; it is the vitality source from which he moves, from which he speaks, from which his critique arises. He is the living presence of divine *being*. He's a human being too, but he's here to convey divine *being*, and that comes out most clearly in the Gospel of Mark.

This gospel uniquely conveys Jesus' search for himself. Mark's Jesus is a Jesus who is very much a searcher: he's looking for his identity, he's looking for his role, he's experimenting, he's finding out what works and what doesn't. He's on a journey, and he's inviting all of us along for that journey with him as if we were also the disciples.

Of all the Gospels, as I mentioned, Mark most clearly shows us Jesus the spiritual revolutionary. In this gospel, Jesus has an almost bitter rejection of corruption at any level; he's a critic of the religion that he was brought up in. Jesus is a Jew from the beginning to the end of the story; he is born a Jew and he dies a Jew. He never rejects his religion, but he does seek to revolutionize it.

Jesus did what all real prophets do, which is to breathe new life and new spirit into the old ways and the old stories. He transformed them into something that really speaks to the heart, to that within us that seeks a relationship with the radiance of divinity and also ultimately seeks to become and embody that radiance. Ultimately, the sole concern of Jesus as depicted in the Gospel of Mark is with awakening people to eternal life, to discovering divine *being* within themselves.

There are two themes that run throughout this entire gospel. One of them is Jesus' evolving role—how he sees himself, how he transmits his teaching, how through the story he evolves his understanding of his role in life. The other theme has to do with what constitutes a correct relationship with divine *being*. By that I mean: How to be in the right relationship to the divinity within ourselves? What is the correct and useful way to approach the mystery of our own existence? These two themes are at the center of what the entire Gospel of Mark expresses.

MATTHEW, LUKE, AND JOHN

Even though Mark provides my central inspiration and interpretive lens, I'll also explore material from all the other Gospels. The Gospel of Matthew uses about eighty percent of the material that we find in the Gospel of Mark, but Matthew adds a lot too; Matthew is fifty percent longer than Mark. Matthew's emphasis in his gospel is with the community of churches and how the spirit of the Jesus story relates to the churches. As a result, the Gospel of Matthew is probably the favorite gospel of preachers. In this gospel, Jesus is presented as the good shepherd, as the loving and welcoming presence of *being*. Of course we still find the revolutionary Jesus in Matthew, but this added sense of Jesus as the embodiment of love really shines through in Matthew, and that's why this gospel has been so popular over the years.

The Gospel of Luke sees Jesus as the fulfillment of the Old Testament prophecies. Luke was speaking to a much wider audience than Matthew, and we sense that as we read the Gospel of Luke. The story has a more universal feel, in order to reach beyond the particular Jewish culture of the time and connect with the gentiles.

In Matthew and Luke we get the Sermon on the Mount, in Matthew the Beatitudes. This is the Jesus that most people imagine: Jesus the good shepherd, a beautiful, openhearted well of compassion and infinite love. That aspect of Jesus will be brought out too, because the transmission of infinite love is a very important part of the story.

THE GOSPEL OF JOHN

The Gospel of John is the most mystical of the Gospels. The Gospel of John sees Jesus as the creative principle, as that which is the spirit or animating force of all of life. Jesus takes on a very transcendent quality; he's much more of an abstraction in the Gospel of John. He's magisterial, beyond everything that seems to be happening to him; the tragic element of his story doesn't ever seem to affect him.

It's a very different portrayal than any of the other Gospels. John wasn't nearly as interested in Jesus' humanity as he was in Jesus' divinity. In fact, in John, the figure of Jesus usurps the entire Old Testament, and Jesus becomes the principle of creation itself. John begins his gospel, "In the beginning was the Word, and the

Word was with God, and the Word was God." [John 1:1, NIV, ESV] Later, we'll explore what John means by the Word, but as you read this gospel you get the feeling that the humanity of Jesus is fully transcendent.

John's Jesus is a very expansive figure of divinity that evokes our own divinity: that which was never touched by the world of time and space, that within you that was constant through all the difficult or tragic moments of your life as the witness to them all, that which never fully enters the world of time, that which is always transcendent of everything that will ever happen. That is a very liberating aspect of divine *being* also and a key part of what John wanted to convey.

THE GOSPEL OF THOMAS

The last gospel that I draw upon is the Gospel of Thomas. Now, the Gospel of Thomas is not found within the Bible. In fact, it was only discovered in 1945, in a clay jar in the desert in Nag Hammadi, Egypt. Often, the Gospel of Thomas is thought of as a Gnostic gospel, but it's only Gnostic in the sense that all the teaching is meant to awaken us from our identification with body and mind and ego to the Kingdom of Heaven, to divinity within. In ancient times, this experience would be called a moment of *gnosis,* of awakening.

The Gospel of Thomas differs from the four Gospels of the New Testament in that it portrays Jesus as a teacher. In the Gospel of Thomas, there is no narrative of Jesus' life, only a collection of brief teachings. These sayings of Jesus are sometimes obviously instructive, but at other times they function more like a Zen koan. A koan is a riddle that you cannot solve with your dualistic conceptual mind; you actually have to move into a state of spiritual awakening in order to understand it.

The Gospel of Thomas presents the Kingdom of Heaven as something that exists right here and right now. In fact, it's all about what's right here and right now. In it, we find Jesus saying, "The Kingdom of the Father is spread out upon the earth, and men do not see it." [Gospel of Thomas 113] This gospel's immediacy offers a challenge to us, as if it's saying down through the centuries, "Have your eyes opened? Can you see divinity right now, right where you are? Can you see the transcendent light shining through the world of time and space?" The Gospel of Thomas is an invitation to find the unique signature of divinity in our lives.

The Gospel of Thomas also focuses on our identity. What we find in both the Old and New Testaments is an emphasis on our relationship with God, with the transcendent deity. The emphasis is on having a proper relationship with God. Of course, in the New Testament Gospels there are times when Jesus goes beyond relationship, as when he says, "You are the light of the world." There are moments in the canonical Gospels when Jesus is very clearly talking about discovering the true depths of our own identity as the universal eternal presence of *being*. But in the Gospel of Thomas, the whole point of Jesus' teaching is to discover your true identity, to realize who and what you really and truly are *here and now*. So I feel that the Gospel of Thomas completes the Jesus story; it widens our picture of what Jesus was and what he had to reveal to us.

In *Resurrecting Jesus,* as we explore the Jesus story, I'll be pulling from each of the Gospels at different times, with the Gospel of Mark as my primary motif and inspiration.

IF JESUS WERE ALIVE TODAY

I often wonder what would it be like if Jesus were alive today. Imagine Jesus—who wasn't a Christian, after all, but a

Jew—entering a church today, going up to the pulpit and giving a sermon. Can you imagine how challenging that would be for the congregation? Can you imagine how uniquely different that sermon would be from what many of us received in church?

In the Gospels, Jesus repeatedly challenges the religious authorities of the day, but ultimately what he's saying is relevant to *all* forms of religion. It wouldn't matter if he grew up a Jew, or a Christian, or a Buddhist, or a Hindu, because he's speaking about the structure of religion itself—its hierarchy, its tendency to become corrupted by human beings' desires for power, for influence, for money. Jesus, I think, had a profound understanding that the religion itself, instead of connecting us to the radiance of being, connecting us to that spiritual mystery, could easily become a barrier to divinity. As soon as we get too caught up with the rites and the rituals and the *Thou shalts* and *Thou shalt nots* of conventional religion, we begin to lose sight of the primary task of religion, which is to orient us toward the mystery of *being* and awaken us to what we really are.

Of course, these external forms do have a certain usefulness. The social function of religion is to have a moderating influence on egoic impulses and desires, and this moral and ethical role has been very important throughout history. When people move in the world of time and space from a healthy sense of ethics and morals, it's a very positive thing, and religion has an important function in helping control the deeper and darker impulses of the ego.

But religion's primary function is not about conveying ethical and moral codes, not about politics and power and hierarchy. Religion's primary function is to awaken within us the experience of the sublime and to connect us with the mystery of existence. As soon as religion forgets about its roots in the eternal, it fails in its central task. Jesus was so critical of the religion of his time because he saw that not only was it not connecting people to the mystery, but that it was actually an active participant in veiling the mystery of existence, in obscuring the Kingdom of Heaven. And so he was a critic from the *inside;* he didn't necessarily reject the religion he was brought up in, but he felt called to challenge it, to transform it. Jesus' keen insight into the potential for the corrupting influence of power in all institutions—whether they're political, economic or religious—is very relevant to the modern day. If Jesus existed here and now as a human being, what he'd have to say about these subjects would be as shocking now as it was two thousand years ago.

I've talked to many people over many years that have turned away from Christianity because it seems so often to focus on only the moral and ethical questions, on telling them how to live their lives, but hasn't connected with them in a really deep way. Of course, there are those churches today that are inspired by the real living presence of Christ, but as a whole, Christianity needs new life breathed into it. It needs to be challenged to awaken from the old structures that confine spirit, so that the perennial spirit of awakening can flourish once again.

This may bring a sense of insecurity, but the living presence of the Christ is something that can't be contained within any structure. The spirit that Jesus embodies is not a safe spirit; there's no guarantee of how it will all play out in your life. There's only one guarantee that Jesus gave: if you can receive and awaken and embody what he is speaking about, then your life will never be the same again. Then you will realize that you're already living in the Kingdom of Heaven.

The Jesus story gives us many different images of how spiritual realization can be embodied in the world of time and space. It's important for us to realize that we must not only have the courage to recognize the divinity within ourselves, but also to embody it and manifest it in the way we live. Jesus as a living presence is not meek or mild. Jesus was a revolutionary, but he wasn't a revolutionary just for the sake of rebellion; he wanted to break down the lines of separation between people, between heaven and earth, between human and divine.

The events in the Jesus story can be seen as a living metaphor for what's necessary in our own *being*. The true boundaries that need to be broken down are the boundaries within our own minds and within our own hearts. So the whole Jesus story, ultimately, is the map of a journey that happens within *us*. It's an invitation to live out the radiance that's revealed when we have the courage to step beyond anything and everything that separates us.

THE DEEP TRUTH
OF MYTH

> Life is this simple: we are living in a world
> that is absolutely transparent and the divine
> is shining through it all the time. This is not
> just a nice story or a fable, it is true.
>
> THOMAS MERTON

In contemporary Western culture, we have become illiterate in the language of myth. We've forgotten all about the truth myths can carry, the significance that they can transmit. In the modern age, most people understand myth simply as something that's not factually true, and that's a profound misunderstanding of myth. Myth isn't about factual or historical truth, but about a deeper truth. In ancient times, people saw myth in a very different light—as a vehicle that can transmit and carry a subtlety and richness of experience that simply cannot be conveyed by linear, conceptual forms of language.

To get a sense of the limits of conceptual language, let me give you an example. I could, for instance, try to describe to you what an orange tastes like. I could tell you that it's sweet, that it has a tinge of sourness, that it's juicy, that the juice explodes in your mouth when you bite into it. I could tell you everything I know about an orange, but at the end of the day, even if I spend an hour describing the taste, you won't really know at all what an orange tastes like until you have bitten into one yourself.

So even something as simple as the taste of a piece of fruit can't be conveyed through our linear way of speaking. Of course, the most powerful way of conveying it is through direct experience, and this is what spirituality is really all about—evoking in you a direct experience of what the outer forms of spirituality are pointing toward. But there is also a way of conveying, at a very deep and subtle level, truths, realities, and experiences that can't be expressed through logical or factual language. The language of myth is multivalenced, metaphorical, and allusive; it operates on many levels at once. In ancient times, people understood that myth and story can carry much more subtlety and richness of experience than mere facts. Today, much of this understanding has been lost, and this is really unfortunate, because it has cut us off from the richness that a mythic way of interpreting a story has to offer.

Spiritual truths cannot be conveyed by facts. Facts are useful for practical purposes; if your plane leaves at three o'clock from a certain airport, you need to know that or you'll miss your plane. But when you're trying to convey deeper meaning, to convey the understanding that can come as a result of experiencing the sublime, you need a different mode of communication. That mode of communication historically has been the myth, the story.

So it's really important that we hear the Jesus story with the ears of myth and metaphor. In fact, many of the Christian mystics read the Jesus story very metaphorically—though it would have been dangerous at times for them to say this directly. It was through this mythic reading that they gained access to the true gift of the story, which is the mystery of existence: the mystery of *your* existence, the mystery of Jesus' existence, and the mystery of God's existence.

Now, many people think of these biblical narratives that make up the Jesus story as strictly factual and historical. For some, it's an article of faith to take every word in the bible as the word of God. I'm not going to argue with those who see it that way, but if one can *also* see it mythically, it can reveal new meanings. So whether we see the Jesus story as fact or myth or a combination of both doesn't really matter. It's helpful simply to peer into the mythical orientation, into that deep sense of storytelling that our ancestors knew so intimately.

Our modern understanding of myth as untruth has left us confused about the function of myth. Myth is not the opposite of fact. It is an invitation for each of us to enter into a story while teasing out its metaphorical and symbolic meaning. What myth carries is not fact, not history, but truth—the ultimate reality. The Jesus story carries this ultimate reality, and that's why, two thousand years later, it remains so compelling.

THE GOD-MAN

In Christian theology, Jesus is both God and man. Now, many of the world's spiritual traditions have their own versions of the God-man, and in the vast majority there is very little humanity left in the God-man character. One of the amazing things about the Jesus story is that, when you read the Gospels, you find that this God-man retains some very human characteristics.

When I was growing up, the cultural expression of Jesus made him seem much more God than man to me. He seemed magisterial, floating above everything that happened in the story. But when I opened up the New Testament and I started to read, I was surprised to find a character that had a very dynamic quality of inner development.

When we think of our humanity, we think of what we feel and how we react to the events in our lives. People have good days and bad days, they have upsets, they have joys, they have sorrows, and this whole spectrum of experience makes up our humanity. In Jesus, the quality of divinity is obviously important, but the quality of humanity is important as well. Jesus is perhaps the only God-man figure in all of religion that we can really identify with: he has his good days, he has his bad days, he experiences happiness, and he experiences sorrow.

For an example of Jesus' deep humanity, take the moment in the Garden of Gethsemane when it suddenly dawns on him that he is going to be crucified. At first, he's distraught, even frightened. He begs God to relieve him of having to go through this experience, saying "Father . . . everything is possible for you. Take this cup from me." [Mark 14:36, NIV] Essentially, he's asking, "Do I really have to go through with this?" These kinds of human characteristics are not often found in the God-men of religion.

As I read through the gospel story, I found this mixture of divinity and humanity really compelling. It connected with me as a human being because I saw those same qualities in my own experience. My own spiritual development has shown me that we're all, in essence, the divine radiance of pure *being* and that we also have our human side: our good days and our not-so-good days. Our human condition is reflected in the great humanity of Jesus, and I believe this is one of the reasons that so many people have felt so deeply connected to Jesus over the centuries.

Reading the Gospels, I was struck by the quality of vitality in Jesus, especially in contrast to how the Buddha is presented in Buddhism. The iconic image of the Buddha is seated in full lotus position, meditating. It's an image meant to convey the sense of eternity experienced when we touch upon the deepest nature of our *being*. Once again, eternity is peering through the latticework of time and space, and this sense of eternal stillness and deep freedom is what the iconic image of the seated Buddha conveys. What this image doesn't convey is a sense of humanity, of a real flesh-and-blood human being. But in the Jesus story, it's as if the still point that the image of the Buddha evokes within us becomes a very dynamic engagement with life.

THE IMAGE OF THE CRUCIFIXION

The most iconic image from the Jesus story, of course, is of Jesus being crucified on the cross. It's very unusual for the God-man of any religion to have as their iconic image a vision of suffering and death—though of course the crucifixion opens the way for the resurrection.

This image deeply connects to our humanity. We're not being nailed to crosses today, and that's a really fortunate thing, but most people who have lived a few decades will have found their own way of experiencing a type of crucifixion. There is a tragic element to human existence for all of us—moments of life when you feel completely overwhelmed or at your wit's end. Whether we want to acknowledge it or not, whether we're running away from it or we're engaged in spirituality in an effort to transcend it, nonetheless, that tragic element of life exists. It can take many forms: a terminal illness, a parent losing their child, a child losing their parent, a husband losing his wife, the death of a friend, losing a job, getting divorced. These are the moments when life bites back.

There are only two certainties about life: that you will some-day die and that between birth and death you will encounter tragedy. I think people associate the iconic image of Jesus on the cross with a certain kind of tragedy: when you're pushed beyond your limits, when everything that you might have believed in breaks down, and in that moment nothing comes to rescue you, nothing comes to save you, and yet nonetheless you have to go through with the experience.

Ultimately, there's a triumph through meeting the tragic elements of life. From one perspective, the entire Jesus story reads like a Greek tragedy, but the beauty of the story is in how it reveals that sense of eternity, that still point in the midst of difficulty, that divinity shining through the latticework of time and space.

The story of Jesus has a triumphant ending, but it's essentially a tragic story—yet through the tragedy shines this radiance of eternal *being*. As Jesus says, "The Kingdom of the Father is spread out upon earth, and men do not see it." [Gospel of Thomas 113] That is an extraordinary statement from someone who has had to live through such tragedy. Jesus is saying that the Kingdom of Heaven is right *here*, in the place where he's undergoing his trials, and men do not see it. The beauty of the Jesus story is that he *did* see eternity while here on this earth; he *was* eternity, divine *being* at his core and in his substance.

Jesus was divinity having a human experience. Whether we have realized this in our own experience or whether we just intuitively connect to it, there is a way that we can sense this divinity showing through the world of time. There is a sense of meaning throughout all of life; there is a sense of radiance.

The Jesus story is both a tragedy and a triumph, and that's why it connects to our lives. In fact, the triumph and the tragedy are intimately locked together throughout the whole of the Jesus story, from the very beginning to the very end. It doesn't begin in tragedy and end in triumph; these two elements are inextricably entwined. The story connects in a nuanced way with both our humanity and our divinity.

THE SPIRITUAL MYSTERY THAT WE ARE

Whomever Jesus may or may not have been historically, he symbolizes the spiritual mystery of each one of us. We are all divine *being* manifesting as human being. Jesus represents that radiance of divine *being,* that felt sense of eternity within us all. When we look back over the arc of our lives, from the time we were born to the present moment, each of us can touch upon that intuition that there's something about us that is unchanged. Throughout all of the ups and downs and changes of life, something is now as it ever was. To touch upon this is to begin to experience eternity within.

Through the whole trajectory from birth to childhood to adolescence and then into adulthood, we change so much, not only physically but also emotionally and intellectually, yet something remains unchanged. That sense of something unchanged is the eternal spark within. At the beginning it may be felt as a very subtle, almost incomprehensible intuition, but when we bring our full attention to that felt intuition of what's the same throughout our whole lives, then that little seed of divine radiance can begin to reveal itself, can begin to shine brighter and brighter in our lives.

I believe that the character and presence of Jesus has something very important to show us in this regard—that each one of us is the son or the daughter of God. As the great fourteenth-century Catholic mystic, Meister Eckhart said, "The Father gives birth to his Son without ceasing; and I say more: He gives birth to me, his Son and the same Son."

That's an extraordinarily bold statement and bolder because he said it in the fourteenth century, where the church still had the power to burn you at the stake or to imprison you if you were found guilty of heresy. And yet Meister Eckhart had the courage to come forth and say that he and Christ are one and the same son. This is the perennial mystic revelation of awakening to our true nature, at one with the divine. When we begin to embody in a deep way the spirit of Jesus we find in the story, then we might begin to feel and sense and experience ourselves becoming that presence and know that presence is actually something that lives within ourselves. The Jesus story is a means of activating the living presence of our *being,* so that we realize that each one of us is the son or daughter of the living God.

In the Gospel of Thomas, Jesus says, "There is light within a man of light, and he lights up the whole world." [Gospel of Thomas 24] That light within us all is that which you intuit when you sense that something about you has remained unchanging throughout all the days of your life. If you put your attention on it, if you meditate upon it in stillness, it can open up and reveal that indeed it is the divine light, that which lights up the whole world. In fact, the more awake we become to our own divinity, the more we feel revitalized by a living presence, by that which reveals that life is sacred. Human life is sacred; all of life is sacred.

Jesus concludes that passage in the Gospel of Thomas by saying, "If he does not shine, he is darkness." That's the challenge. That's the Jesus who tells it to us straight, who doesn't water down the message. Either we are in light or we are in darkness. That's a teaching meant to shake us from our slumber. In order to come into our full potential and to embody the truth and radiance of what we are, we must come vitally alive; we must lean once again into presence; we must pour ourselves forth into life, instead of trying to escape life and avoid its challenges. Then our lives themselves become expressions of love, of overflow, because we have compassionately given ourselves to life, to our incarnation, as a means to redeem it—to bring everything home, back to its source, to the eternal radiance within each and every one of us.

A MAP OF AWAKENING 4

> If a man wishes to be sure of the road he treads
> on, he must close his eyes and walk in the dark.
>
> ST. JOHN OF THE CROSS

The Jesus story reads like a roadmap for spiritual awakening.
The journey of awakening to divine *being* that you and I can
realize internally, Jesus lived out in his life story, through his
humanity. This is one of the amazing things about the Jesus story.
If you've gone through the steps and stages of awakening, you
cannot help but to see these stages embodied in the Jesus story.

The Jesus story doesn't directly address spiritual awakening because it's speaking in mythic language, the language of
metaphor. In order to understand the story being told in the
Gospels, you literally need to absorb it, to *become* it. You can't
remain a spectator and expect to understand it, because then
you're on the outside, still stuck in the logical, linear mind. The
truths being conveyed through the Jesus story are beyond logic,

beyond the conditioned thinking mind; they're of a higher order of wisdom that you can only really understand by awakening.

THE CALLING

The first stage of the awakening journey is the calling. The calling arrives when we first feel that spiritual impulse that galvanizes our attention. All of a sudden we sense a greater mystery to life that we seek to experience more deeply; it literally calls us.

Through my teaching, I have heard many people's stories of their calling. Sometimes it happens in childhood as a result of a spiritual opening experience that reorients their life. They may forget about that story for years or even decades, only to remember it later in life and then connect the dots, seeing that the opening they experienced as a child changed the course of their life. This calling can arrive at any point in your life. It is that moment when the trajectory of your life begins to turn toward the mystery of life. When I say *the mystery of life*, what I'm referring to is that transcendent aspect of life that shines through the world of space and time.

Now, if we're completely caught up in our dualistic mind and not paying close attention, then we don't even notice that this spiritual core of existence is shining through into the world of time. But most people don't begin to experience this or even know it's there until something in their life opens them enough that they begin to experience the sublime. It may be a great moment, it may be small, but when that moment of significance reveals to you that there's more to life than you imagined, there's more to *you* than you imagined, that is the beginning of the calling. From that moment on, your life is now on a different trajectory than it was before.

I can remember when this happened to me. Now, I had spiritual interests my whole life, but I didn't really feel this calling, where the orientation of life shifts quite suddenly, until I was about twenty years old. As I described earlier, I'd picked up a book on Zen Buddhism and come upon the word *enlighten-ment*. At the time, I didn't know what enlightenment was. I'd hardly even heard of it, and I certainly never thought that I was going to seek enlightenment. But when I read that word on the page, it was like a little nuclear explosion inside of me. It evoked something in me so powerful that I knew that the trajectory of my life, at the instant that I read that word, was forever changed.

It was not something that I sought; it was not something that I wanted or even tried to make happen: it simply happened, and the trajectory of my life was never the same from that point on. I remember getting up the next morning feeling scared and excited. I had a conversation with my mother in which I told her, "You know, the trajectory of my life has *completely* shifted overnight." I described what had happened, she gave me the sense that she had some understanding of what I was talking about, and she was very supportive.

As with any good adventure, I felt excited that a new vista of my life had opened up, full of possibility and mystery, but also I had a little bit of fear, because I realized that I had no control over what had happened. I didn't make the calling happen, I couldn't pretend it didn't happen, and I couldn't have turned it off even if I'd wanted to. It was disconcerting. And sure enough, my intuition was true: the entire trajectory of my life had changed at that instant.

That's the calling. Mine was pretty obvious, while for others it's more subtle. It occurs within each person in a unique way, so it doesn't necessarily have to be felt as a big event: it can just be that moment when you open to the transcendent quality of life. Then, you often find yourself drawn to some sort of spiritual path. In my case, I found a Zen teacher and spent the next fourteen years with her, meditating and studying.

THE AWAKENING

The next phase of one's spiritual life is the awakening, and the word *awakening* is quite accurate. When you have a dream in the middle of the night, at the moment you wake from your dream, you suddenly realize, "Oh, it was a dream!" Yet the moment before you woke up, the dream was entirely real to you. It was as real as this moment. You wake up from the reality of the dream space to the reality of your everyday life, your waking mindset.

In the same way, spiritual awakening occurs when you awaken from what you *think* of as your normal state of consciousness—awake, eyes open, moving about in the world—to your deep, essential, true nature. It literally feels like waking from a dream. It's as if you wake up from the dream of thinking that you're already awake in your ordinary waking state. When you are spiritually awakened, what you *thought* was an awake state now seems like a dream.

There's a shift from one order of reality to another. In a certain sense, the center of your regard shifts from yourself as a separate person to that which unifies us all. That's really what spiritual awakening is: a shift from seeing yourself as a limited, isolated, separate person to realizing you are essentially that which all beings partake of, that which all beings essentially and truly are. After awakening, that deeper sense of reality is available to you and your sense of who you are, your identity has undergone a transformation.

The esoteric, inner spiritual disciplines of all traditions are means of bringing about this awakening or of opening one to awakening. This is what occurs at the very beginning of the Gospel of Mark, when John the Baptist baptizes Jesus in the River of Jordan. "Just as Jesus was coming up out of the water, he saw heaven being torn open and the spirit descending on him like a dove." [Mark 1:10, NIV] When you awaken, when spirit descends, the veil of your dream state is torn apart, and all of a sudden you're awakened to a new reality.

The words used to describe the spirit descending into Jesus after his baptism correspond very closely with one of my own experiences. Often, this awakening is a transcendent experience; you awaken up and out of your identity with body and mind. In my case, I had that experience too, a very powerful experience of moving up and out. Spirit or consciousness literally moved up and out of the body and the mind, and for a period of time there was absolutely no experience of anything. The body was gone. The mind was gone. I had no perception of the world or my surroundings; I had moved into a total void.

From that state of voidness, after a while a download of insight began—literally hundreds of insights per second downloaded into my system. Just as you download a program on your computer, spirit or divine *being* was downloading insights into me, many more than I could actually keep up with. This descent of spirit was just as depicted in the Jesus story.

As I said, I'm reading the Jesus story as a metaphor for spiritual awakening. If you have experienced the descent of spirit, you know exactly what this passage in Mark is talking about. You don't need anybody to confirm it; you *know.* You know that the story tells of the descent of spirit in as clear a way as it can be told, that the metaphor mirrors the actual experience.

There are many degrees of awakening, but *all* awakening has as its common denominator a shift from seeing ourselves as a separated, isolated human being to seeing ourselves as that which we all share. You can call it consciousness, divine *being,* spirit, God. Many words can be used, but it's the experience that matters.

TRIALS AND TRIBULATIONS

At some point after awakening—sometimes very soon, sometimes not for quite a while—you reach a stage that I call "trials
and tribulations." In the Jesus story, this is symbolized by Jesus'
forty days in the desert and his encounter with Satan in the desert immediately following his baptism. In Buddhism, this stage
is mythically portrayed by the image of Buddha sitting under
the bodhi tree, assaulted by Maya, the force of illusion. Maya is
an impersonal force of illusion, while Satan is a personification
of what we think of as evil, but the source of evil is actually illusion, so these are really two different mythic representations of
the same experience.

When it comes to human beings, however, things are usually not quite as simple as they're portrayed in the images of
myth, because our experience is so nuanced and subtle that it's
difficult to convey in a story. But at this stage, each of us will
likely undergo a series of trials, lasting months or even years.
Through these trials, our new state of consciousness is put to
the test by situations that we encounter in life that will test the
depth of our realization. It's almost as if life says, in order to deal
with this situation properly, you are going to have to respond
to it from that place of realization, from your deepest nature to
which you've awakened. If you go back into your ego or into
your conditioned mind to respond, it simply won't work, and
turmoil will ensue.

As we go through our trials and tribulations, outer circumstances seem to be exquisitely put together specifically to test
each part of our realization. These trials and tribulations will
also occur from the inside. Your unconscious at some point
will start to reveal itself. In the unawakened person, the unconscious never fully comes into conscious awareness, but with
awakening our means of suppression and denial are either torn

apart completely or wounded so severely that we can't repress as much. The unconscious elements of our mind come into conscious awareness, and that is another kind of trial. What's being asked of you is to meet all of that inner material from the standpoint of divine *being,* from the standpoint of eternity—to meet it, to understand it, to resolve it. That may sound quite easy, but when it's actually happening it's a little more gritty and real than the description suggests.

You could think of these inward and outward trials as a form of purification. You're purifying the vehicle: body and mind, the same body and mind that you woke up out of when you awakened. Now this vehicle has to undergo its own purification so spirit can fully embody your humanity. And this is where the story of Jesus again provides a powerful mirror, because Jesus is someone who embodied in his humanity the divine impulse, divine *being.*

As Jesus moves through his story, from beginning to end, he encounters almost nothing *but* trials and tribulations. How does he meet each one of these challenges, from Satan in the desert all the way to the crucifixion? From what place inside does he act? You'll see that Jesus is uncompromising; he always acts from the truth of eternal *being.* This is an amazing teaching, and it's message is: if you meet your trials and tribulations from your own deepest realization, they will be released from your system and purified from you, so that eternal *being* can fully be embodied through your humanity.

ABIDING TRANQUILITY

The next stage of awakening is what I call "abiding tranquility." Abiding tranquility arises when, through the purification process of the body and mind initiated by the trials and tribulations, your humanity is literally emptied of conflict. What follows is an inner state of unification. All the forces in you are now unified: your psychology, your spirit, your will. The personal will is no longer pushing and pulling you all over the place, and you no longer have a constant sense of psychological and spiritual friction; instead, there is a deep state of abiding tranquility.

Now, this doesn't mean you're always tranquil; you are still capable of utilizing the full spectrum of human emotion. But the inner, underlying reality is a very obvious abiding tranquility, and when there's real unification, nothing can pull you out of it. You might go through challenging times, but essentially, in the depth of your *being*, you're unified. And when you're unified inside, then you also see unification on the outside—because the inner and the outer are actually one thing.

Now, this phase of abiding tranquility is not really evident in the Jesus story until the end, in part because it doesn't make for good storytelling. Abiding tranquility is something that we associate with the Buddha seated in his meditation posture; it's a symbol for something that exists as a potential within all of us. The Buddha image shows us abiding tranquility amidst the turning wheel of life. The Jesus story is not focused on finding within yourself that still point around which the dualistic world turns, but on how that tranquility *functions* in the world of time and space. So we don't really get the image of this still point during the Jesus story. It's all happening so fast and furious, one event right after the other, that this abiding tranquility phase isn't discernible except for the fact that Jesus' actions are expressions of it.

But even though it isn't highlighted in the story, it is a key part of the journey of awakening. When this unification occurs, there's a simplicity to life, a deep sense of freedom and essential well-being and also of fearlessness. Fearlessness doesn't mean the same thing as courage, because one is only courageous in the face of fear. Instead it comes as a sense of immovability, a feeling that nothing is driving you or compelling you onward. It can feel very much like the culmination of spiritual awakening—but it's not.

THE TRANSFIGURATION

For the next phase of the journey, I use the same name by which it's known in the Gospels—"the transfiguration." In the Jesus story, the transfiguration occurs upon a high mountain where Jesus has gone with three of his disciples. The Gospel of Matthew reads, "There he was transfigured before them. His face shone like the sun, and his clothes became as white as the light." [Matthew 17:2, NIV] In that moment, Jesus becomes radiant light. Obviously, in the Jesus story the transfiguration happens in a very striking manner. In most people's lives, it's not going to be quite that extraordinary.

If we see it in a more human way, the transfiguration conveys a deepening of one's realization. Where there was abiding tranquility, what awakens now is sense of an extraordinary vitality, of life-force. It's as if the fullness of your *being* is radiating, and from the tips of your toes to the top of your head, you feel this very deep and powerful radiance.

And it does change you inside. When you've been in a state of abiding tranquility and then you're infused with this impersonal vitality and radiance, very often it signals that there's something more in store. There will be another phase of your life, a phase not just of abiding tranquility, but also of radiant engagement.

There's an interesting parallel between the transfiguration of Jesus and the Old Testament story of Moses and the burning bush. [Exodus 3] Like Jesus, Moses has gone up the mountain. There, he's met by the burning bush, a bush filled with radiance from which God speaks to Moses. In the Old Testament, Moses encounters God in the burning bush, but Moses is still Moses and God is still God. In a culture centered on a tribal God, nothing is more important than God's relationship with the people of the tribe. The Old Testament God can be viewed as a universal tribal god.

In the New Testament, there's a sense in which Jesus usurps Moses. Jesus not only has a *relationship* with the radiance, with the burning, but Jesus himself *becomes* it. That's a significant difference. It's not that one is better than the other: these are both mythic stories, stories mirroring back the potentials within every human being. Within your spiritual journey, you may have a phase of your life where you very much feel like God is *other*, and the goal at that point may be to have the most harmonious, unified relationship you can with God as other. For many people, that's a very important and beautiful part of the journey.

But the Jesus story depicts a different order of experience, one in which you now fully experience yourself to be the divinity. When I say "yourself," I don't mean your ego. If an ego concludes that it's God, that's a very deluded and potentially dangerous ego. It's not your ego that realizes it's God, but your true essence. It might be more accurate to say God within you realizes it's God; the radiance realizes that you are the radiance.

When transfiguration occurs, we begin to move with what I call "spiritual autonomy." By spiritual autonomy, I mean a kind of certainty—not an egoic certainty, but one that comes from your essential nature, from the level of divine *being*. We find this spiritual autonomy very clearly mirrored in the figure of Jesus. Jesus walks through his life knowing who he is and what he's doing, even though his disciples don't understand him, the authorities don't understand him, and the Pharisees don't understand him. At times it seems like the whole world is against him, but he knows what his mission is, and nothing and nobody is going to get in the way of that. He lives that mission out unto his death. The price he pays for that autonomy is his own life.

This is a mythic portrayal of what spiritual autonomy looks like and how it moves in the world of time and space. It's not even trying to make the egoic perspective understand it or agree with it; it is its own dominion, its own sovereignty. It's going to do what it's going to do, and the egoic state of consciousness literally has no capacity whatsoever to understand it, because this autonomy is functioning from a different dimension of *being*.

Jesus spoke of being *in* the world, but not *of* the world; this is real spiritual autonomy in action. I believe Jesus displays and mirrors back this autonomy better than any other character in any spiritual story or myth that I've ever read or encountered.

RELINQUISHMENT

The next stage of the awakening journey is what I call "relinquishment." In the story of Jesus, relinquishment is symbolized by the crucifixion. Ultimately, relinquishment is the experience of the death of ego.

Awakening is the transcendence of ego; awakening doesn't mean the ego is dead or even that it's really gone anywhere. The awakening experience may change the nature of ego, making it more unified, more whole, but the ego is still there. Relinquishment is what spiritual teachers mean when they say, "die before you die." Many people mistake "dying before you die" with spiritual awakening, because awakening can feel like a death and rebirth process. But this relinquishment is something much, much deeper; in it, the egoic self actually dies, and afterward you operate from a different place, a place without a center.

This is graphically portrayed in the crucifixion. In the Gospel of Mark, the last words you hear from Jesus are "My God, my God, why have you forsaken me?" [Mark 15:34, NIV, ESV] and then his life ends with a death scream. This is Jesus' humanity, feeling completely and absolutely abandoned by God. This is a very dynamic portrayal of an actual inward experience.

Of course, you can read the crucifixion on many different levels, and I mentioned earlier how moments of difficulty, sorrow, and tragedy in life can correspond to the crucifixion. But here I'm speaking about the crucifixion as a stage of the spiritual journey. Ego death feels like a death, it's experienced as a death, and usually the ego doesn't go easily. Of course, the ego's fundamental identity is that it is separate: separate from life, separate from others and, religiously speaking, separate from God. This is what Jesus experiences in his last moments: the last vestige of the separate self, screaming out its confession, "I have been forsaken." This is what the state of separation *feels* like—like being forsaken. We can only imagine how this last remaining sense of separation comes out of nowhere for Jesus there on the cross, as he lives out his humanity through the spiritual journey. From another perspective, he's already been through all this. Thus, in the very beginning he descends from heaven to live the journey out so that you and I have this story that mirrors it back to us.

THE TRANSMUTATION

The very last phase of spiritual awakening is what I call "the transmutation." Transmutation is what transfiguration and relinquishment make possible. In it, your orientation to life is entirely selfless. It's not that you *want to* be selfless or you're practicing being selfless: rather you're selfless in the sense of no self.

For this transition to happen, one has to go through the death of the ego. Certain aspects of the transmutation may occur earlier in our own journey, but the crucifixion or relinquishment must be complete for it to happen in full. At that point, really, the only thing left to do is to be a selfless, benevolent presence in the world—there's really nothing else to do, nothing else that makes sense. Whatever that may look like—and it looks different for different people—that's where the whole process ends up.

In the Jesus story, this stage is termed the resurrection. Out of death is resurrected a new life, which really means a new orientation. That movement, that long turning from self-orientation to selfless orientation now comes to fruition. This is where the journey culminates for Jesus, and this is where it ultimately culminates for anyone who's taken the journey of awakening.

REDEEMING YOUR HUMAN INCARNATION

The story of Jesus mirrors back the journey of spiritual awakening for anyone who has the eyes to see it or the experience to notice it. I believe this is among the most powerful lenses through which to view the story, because from this perspective the story begins to live and breathe as metaphor.

Jesus doesn't live anything out in a small fashion; everything in his story is writ large. This makes it easier for us to see that he's depicting a journey of awakening. We shouldn't expect to live out our own journey in the same fashion and, fortunately, we don't have to, though our journey will certainly have its own challenges and intensity.

The mystery of the story of Jesus is the same as the mystery of you and me and everyone: we are all God appearing as man and as woman, divine *being* manifesting as human being. They're actually two sides of the same coin. They're one and the same thing; it's only our minds that separate divinity and humanity. We separate them in our mind and in our experience, but the whole spiritual journey is finally to see that they aren't separate, that they never were separate. Even the theology of Jesus bears this out: "For God so loved the world, that he gave his only begotten son." [John 3:16, KJV]

As I tell people when I teach, "God so loved the world, that he sent it his only begotten sons and daughters." That not only applies to Jesus: that's *you*. Imagine if you took it on in yourself to reorient your life trajectory toward your divinity. *Your* divinity: *I so loved the world, that I gave it all of myself*. Imagine your birth as an act of pouring yourself forth into life as a loving means of redemption. Imagine your human life as what you have come to redeem. And when you've fully awakened to all of it, then you've fully redeemed your human incarnation.

Every verse and episode of the Jesus story is a metaphor for the human experience of awakening. This passage may point to a realm of human experience that many people don't experience because they never stop, they never become still, but nonetheless it is there. It is possible to find it in stillness, in silence. As the Bible says, "Be still, and know that I am God." [Psalm 46:10, ESV]

And when you reorient your life toward this realization, then you understand: *you* so loved the world, *you* had so much compassion, *you* had so much love that you poured yourself forth into life, and that pouring forth was your birth. You are here to redeem whatever you encounter in this life, to wake up within everything the deep reality of its divine existence.

The kingdom of heaven is spread upon earth and men do not see it. When you see this, you shift from being a victim of your life and assigning blame for the tragedy you encounter. The truth, I would suggest, is that you poured yourself willingly into form out of infinite love in order to redeem the entirety of this life. When seen from that perspective, all of a sudden life looks very different. You stop holding back from life, your inner life or the life around you, because the kingdom of heaven is within and all around you. *That's* the message of the Jesus story.

TWO

THE JESUS STORY

BIRTH AND BAPTISM

5

> Jesus said, "Blessed is he who came into
> being before he came into being."
>
> **GOSPEL OF THOMAS**

Now we'll begin to explore the Jesus story itself, starting at the very beginning—with the virgin birth. The image of a virgin birth is an ancient mythical motif that existed for more than a thousand years *before* the birth of Jesus, and it signifies something very important within the whole theology of Jesus' incarnation.

THE MEANING OF VIRGIN BIRTH

Theologically, the story of the virgin birth suggests that Jesus descended down to earth from a heavenly state. What is the heavenly state? It is a state that is outside of time. It is a breaking through into eternity. Now, you may have experienced moments of something akin to the heavenly state. There are moments in life when, spontaneously, a door in your consciousness opens and suddenly you see everything from a very different perspective. The doors of perception open and life suddenly takes on the sense of tremendous meaning, even if you can't communicate what that meaning is. The heavenly state is the context of eternity in which the world resides.

Each human being experiences such moments, in which the doors of eternity part—if only a crack—and you're filled with a sense of awe and of joy. When you connect with the infinite mystery of *being,* you sense the immensity of the potential that's within it. So this descent from the heavenly state into the world of time and space is very much tied to these moments where our perception opens and we are connected with the transcendent reality.

In the Jesus story, the virgin birth is that moment when the door cracks open and the spirit of Jesus comes down from the eternal. We should always remember that Jesus represents eternal *being,* that dimension of our own being that is beyond time and space, beyond what we can see and think about and touch. From that perspective, what does it mean that Jesus descends straight from heaven? This is eternal, divine *being* breaking through the latticework of time—breaking through the structures of *our* minds, breaking through *our* belief systems and entering into *our* consciousness.

Now, Jesus is born of a virgin. What does this virgin birth represent? This image is telling us that Jesus is not born of the pairs of opposites. His is a birth straight from heaven, and heaven is eternal wholeness. The virgin birth of Jesus represents heaven taking physical form here on earth. The birth of your physical form is the product of your mother and father, which are the pairs of opposites. But your deeper nature is eternal and not born from the pairs of opposites. It is timeless, and it is birthed into time and space as soon as you have a human incarnation. So there you are, a human being filled with the mystery of eternal *being*, filled with the radiance of spirit.

This is what the virgin birth signifies: time and space being opened up and eternity being embodied as a human being. This is you and I, yet we don't know it. We are eternal, divine beings manifested here and now in our humanity as a particular human being. Our human form comes from the pairs of opposites. The body that feels, the mind that thinks—all this comes from the pairs of opposites. Your mother and father got together and produced a baby, a beautiful, incarnated being, and that being is filled and animated by the vitality of divine *being*. That is the beauty of what the virgin birth signifies if you can read the metaphor.

JESUS' CALLING

The Gospels of Matthew and Luke begin with the birth of Jesus, but the Gospel of Mark begins with Jesus, already a man in his early thirties, seeking out John the Baptist, who has prophesied his coming.

Now, why did Jesus seek out John the Baptist on the shores of the river Jordan? As I have said, for most people the journey of spiritual awakening begins with some sort of calling, some way in which their lives are reoriented toward the mystery, toward a spiritual reality. But in Jesus' case, there's nothing in the story to indicate that he was called, that he was a seeker. Even this is really instructive. I have met a number of people who had no interest in spirituality, who were just going along in their daily lives when all of a sudden: Boom! Out of nowhere they awaken, their spiritual life begins, and they wake up out of who they thought they were to the reality of divine *being*.

Usually we're called; usually we can remember some moment when we began to become aligned with our spiritual search. But there are cases where the calling is skipped and one goes right to the initiation of spiritual awakening. It seems to me that this is what we see when Jesus meets John the Baptist. We're not told whether or not he had a spiritual calling, but we *do* know he specifically sought out John the Baptist. Perhaps he felt a calling to be baptized by John, or perhaps he had a precognition—he knew in some way what his life was going to be all about, and undergoing that initiation of baptism was part of his life's destiny.

THE DOOR BETWEEN TWO WORLDS

John the Baptist is a wild man of sorts. He exists on the fringe of society. He is described as wearing a coat made of camel's hair, and he eats locusts and wild honey. This is someone who operates outside the bounds of society and culture. So John the Baptist represents the unconditioned part of our *being*—of your *being*, of my *being*—that we can connect with if we are courageous enough. It is a part of our *being* that is not conditioned into the mold of society and culture.

Now, the mold in which society and culture form us has a certain usefulness. It tells us how to operate in the world of time and human beings and how to have a certain sense of ethics and morality. This story is talking about something else. It begins with Jesus being baptized by this wild man, outside the bounds of conventional society and religion. This indicates that if you simply follow the route of conventional religion, then you most likely will not penetrate into the deep mystery; you will stay forever on the surface of life. It takes some wildness and risk to penetrate through the surface of a given religious viewpoint and see beyond convention. If we are to find heaven here on earth, we must be willing to open ourselves to the unknown, far beyond where most people will allow themselves to go. So Jesus goes to this man who represents that which is beyond convention, beyond the agreements of the dualistic world.

When Jesus comes to be baptized, John is already widely known. Hordes of people have already come to be baptized by him, and he's obviously a very charismatic figure in his own right. He appealed to that spark of spirit within people, as if to say: Come out beyond the bounds of what is comfortable, of what is known, of what you've been taught. This is the source of vitality, out here in the wild places, in the unknown. This is where spirit is to be discovered.

Now, most people don't embrace this kind of insecurity and don't enter into the unknown within themselves until and unless some traumatic event shakes them so much that they begin to let go of the way they've conceived of life. We tend to hang on to our preconceptions; we tend to hang on to our belief structures, even though they hold us within a very limited frame of perception. But sometimes, in the face of very difficult events—when we face a serious illness or go through divorce or lose a loved one to death—the intensity of our experience puts a crack in our allegiance to the dualistic conditioned perspective, and we may glimpse something of great majesty beyond anything we have ever known.

Most people though, as soon as things return to normal, retreat into their belief systems and conditioned thought structures. But Jesus, in being baptized by John, is going out beyond the world, beyond the confines of the religious structures of his time. He's seeking out someone who can help connect him with the mystery: the mystery that's found in the wild spaces, on the unknown paths that nobody walks, in a place inside that you must go alone or not at all. And so John the Baptist is waiting for Jesus there at the doorway, at the interface between those two worlds. And John the Baptist knows what his role is.

INTO THE MYSTERY

John the Baptist had foretold the coming of Jesus; he knew that something new was coming into the world of time and space, something new and very powerful.

And this was his message: "After me comes one more powerful than I, the straps of whose sandals I am not worthy to stoop down and untie. I baptize you with water, but he will baptize you with the Holy Spirit." [Mark 1:7–8, NIV]

John the Baptist is a wild man, a man outside the confines of organized religion, yet his baptism is the baptism of repentance, of forgiveness. He helps people to release their burdens of their own psychology, of their past. The water in which he baptizes people is purifying water. In many religious traditions, water symbolizes not only purification, but also the moral and ethical dimension of life. When John the Baptist is baptizing people, he's really trying to get them right to that doorway, between the known and the unknown. He wants to purify their vision and clean their souls so they are ready to respond to Jesus when he comes.

The repentance that John the Baptist spoke of can take you right to the boundary line, to those moments where you feel suddenly struck by something strange and compelling that awakens the spirit within you. But the one who's coming after him—the one who turns out to be Jesus—is the one who can pull you through, because he lives on the other side of that imagined boundary. John *shows* the way, but Jesus *is* the way.

Jesus brings a different kind of baptism. As John the Baptist says, "He will baptize you with the Holy Spirit and fire." [Matthew

3:11, NIV, ESV] Now, spirit is associated with breath—to inspire, to breathe in. Spirit is also the animating force; it's the dynamic spiritual force throughout the whole universe. This is where Jesus *came* from. He descended from heaven, from the realm of spirit, and he's able to usher spirit in so that you realize it within yourself. Again, all these qualities exist within oneself: the ethical and moral domain, the boundary between known and the unknown, and finally spirit, which pulls you through the doorway and begins to awaken you into a new dimension of *being*.

If you hear what's being spoken here, you can begin to intuit what these qualities may be like for you. What is that like when you feel like you're taken right to the edge of the unknown? How many times have you pulled back from it only to return, and then pulled back again because it was too unknown, too insecure, too great a risk? Finally, you're compelled to cross that boundary into a new life—a *real* life, a life of vitality, a life of meaning—but not a life you can predict with any certainty and not a life for which society prepares you. Society prepares you for the life *it* wants you to lead; it prepares you for the role that *it* wants you to have. But the spirit within you, unhappy being confined, can compel you to lead a *true* life, a significant life full of the vitality of spirit.

So Jesus comes and is baptized in the water, and at the moment he raises his head the spirit descends into him. As the Gospel of Matthew relates it, "As soon as Jesus was baptized, he went up out of the water. At that moment heaven was opened, and he saw the Spirit of God descending like a dove and alighting on him." [Matthew 3:16, NIV] This descent of the spirit reorients his whole life, gives his life a new direction. From that instant, Jesus' life will never be what it was before. His life will become what we read about in the story. In just this same way, there are moments when you say *yes* to the mystery, when you peer into that dark place, when you realize that you are not what you thought you were—not your beliefs, not your ideas, not the constrictive role that society has placed on you. You are something other than you have been defined as—more other than you can imagine.

And this is what the descent of spirit signifies; it's a way of saying yes to your true nature. But first you have to say yes to the unknown. You have to know that you don't know who you are. You have to know that you don't know what God is. You have to enter into that place where you know that you don't know what life is. You have your ideas and opinions, but you know that those can't really be the truth of you, so you're willing to take the risk. You're willing to step through the veil and enter into the spiritual domain. Taking this step is what Jesus represents. His name for it was *repent*.

Spirit is the symbol for transformation. So when we open to spirit, we're opening to transformation: we're not going to be the same person that began the journey and we're not going to see ourselves in the same way ever again. When we open to spirit, we're not adding a new layer of identity. Spirit is that which throws off all identities and casts them all away. Spirit has no form, no ideology. It is eternal wholeness and completeness.

So what happens when you say *yes* to that invitation? What happens when you metaphorically step off safe ground and into the river and are baptized into the unknown? What is it like to have the heavens part and have eternal spirit descend upon you?

THE AWAKENING TRANSMISSION

Jesus' awakening came in the instant when John baptized him in the river and spirit descended from heaven into him. The role that John the Baptist played in this awakening is fascinating.

John said, "After me comes one who is more powerful than I"; he knew that Jesus had the greater significance, yet John was actually the medium of Jesus' own awakening.

This is a really intimate part of the student-teacher relationship in spirituality. When one has, to some degree, awakened to spirit, the mere fact that one's consciousness is awakened to the spiritual dimension can resonate with others. Then that spiritual dimension will also start to become alive and conscious in them. In spirituality, this is called *transmission*. The image I use for this is of two stringed instruments. If you have two guitars in the same room and pluck a chord on one guitar, the sound waves moving through the air will cause the strings to vibrate sympathetically on the second guitar.

When the teacher's spiritual state begins to resonate with that same reality within the student, then even if the student has not yet awakened to that reality, the teacher's state begins to bring it alive or call it forth. In a certain sense, this is what John was for Jesus: John wasn't Jesus' teacher, as far as we know, but he was the catalyst that opened Jesus up to the descent of spirit.

There has to be a moment when we become available, when we surrender—*ahhhhh*—and our hearts and minds open. In that moment, the transmission of spirit can take place. But you must fully relax; you must have a sense of deep surrender. Otherwise it's as if you were holding your hand against the strings of the guitar. Even if the other guitar is played, your strings won't vibrate. So when we surrender, we become available. It's as if we're taking our hands off the strings; we're taking all suppression off that resonant field within us.

All that life is waiting for is a moment of being still. Then that resonant force can be activated in you, opening you so that spirit can come alive in you. That is a moment of awakening. When spirit comes into you, you see the spiritual reality of your true *being*, your divine nature. You no longer identify yourself with your name, or gender, or occupation, or past history. You know and experience yourself to be pure spirit, the formless and eternal consciousness of all created things. You don't need to *add* divine *being* to yourself; you *are* divine *being* whether you know it or not. You don't become divine *being:* you realize it; you awaken to it. And you awaken to it when you surrender, when you open yourself deeply to another person who's awake or simply to the mystery of life itself.

Just a moment, a split second of true availability is all it takes. That's where spirit gains its entry, and that moment is the moment of awakening. That's what happened to Jesus, right there in the River Jordan when he was baptized by John and the heavens parted. He awakened, and from that point on he preached repentance—to turn around and look within to what it is that is doing the looking. That awakening was the beginning of his new life, the beginning of his mission.

TRIALS AND TRIBULATIONS

6

> To have courage for whatever comes in life—
> everything lies in that.
>
> ST. THERESA OF AVILA

After awakening, we enter into the next phase of the spiritual journey. In awakening, we suddenly recognize our true nature. We recognize that we are not the egoic personality we thought we were, but divine *being,* the radiance of consciousness itself. At some point following this recognition, it's as if the world responds by giving us very specific tests and trials in which we will be asked to engage life from the awakened state, to manifest it and act from it. Realizing the reality of our *being* is one thing, but being able to embody it is something else entirely. The trials and tribulations of life are challenging, but they actually help us begin to act and manifest our realization in the world of time and space, in our daily lives. If we look at the life of Jesus, we see it was one long continuous trial that shows us, time and again, how spirit moves in the world of time and space.

THE FIRST TEMPTATION

Immediately following his awakening, Jesus enters the wilderness to fast for forty days and forty nights. The Gospel of Matthew says, "Then Jesus was led by the Spirit into the wilderness to be tempted by the devil." [Matthew 4:1, NIV] This motif of entering a place of tests and trials is very ancient, very universal. The Buddha had much the same experience under the bodhi tree. The bodhi tree is really symbolic for the tree of life, so the Buddha is sitting in a lush place, quite different than the desert where Jesus goes. Yet he is tempted in equal measure, assaulted by the forces of Maya. In Buddhism, Maya represents illusion; it plays the same role as Satan or the devil in Christianity. The difference is that Maya is the impersonal force of illusion and misunderstanding in the universe; it's not out to destroy you with evil intent. In the Christian story, Satan is the personification of illusion, and because of this Satan takes on a much darker, more sinister quality.

So Jesus is led out into the desert, where he encounters Satan. "After fasting forty days and forty nights, he was hungry. The tempter came to him and said, 'If you are the Son of God, tell these stones to become bread.'" [Matthew 4:2–3, NIV]

Now, imagine that you've fasted for forty days and forty nights; you're going to be tired, you're going to be hungry, you're going to be weak. Along comes this dark force—whether something from outside you or inside you—to tempt you at this moment of weakness. What it essentially says is: I know you're hungry, so if you're really a great awakened being, just do it; just turn those rocks into bread. And Jesus answers Satan, "It is written: 'Man does not live on bread alone, but on every word that comes from the mouth of God.'" [Matthew 4:4, NIV]

This first temptation has to do with the issues of fear and survival, which are really two sides of a single, extraordinarily powerful force. So this first temptation asks us: When you get afraid, when your well-being and even survival are at stake, what do you fall back on? From where do your decisions arise? When you're afraid, do your decisions arise from fear? When you feel threatened, do you respond from your old conditioned sense of self-protection, or do you still maintain a connection with that still point inside—that point of clarity and love inside you where you're not afraid even when you are afraid? The place where love is greater than the instinct to survive?

That place inside allows you to move through your fear, through even the desire to survive. We're often taught that our deepest instinct is the survival instinct, that when push comes to shove, all life forms in the whole universe seek first and foremost to survive. But in human beings at least, we find that this isn't actually the case. There are times in life where people are more than willing to put their lives on the line for someone or something, because there's a love that is deeper than the survival instinct that they can access and function through.

Imagine a parent whose child is out in the middle of the street with a car barreling toward them. You see in an instant that your only chance to save your child is to run out in the street and push them out of harm's way; there's not enough time to carry them to safety. Most parents would run right out in front of the car and push their child out of the way, even if they knew they were going to be struck and killed by the car. Most parents wouldn't even have to think; it would be an instinctive, instantaneous action. At such moments, we have transcended personal survival and tapped into our collective unity.

Something similar, though not as dramatic, occurs when you feel real compassion or sympathy for someone. Each person's experience is his or her own, but when you meet someone who's suffering and you're open to them, available to them, you partake of their experience. Sure, it would be easier for you if you didn't partake of their experience, if you simply closed your heart and didn't have any compassion. But the human heart has a deep capacity for connection. I would suggest that our innate compassion arises from the intuition that we are not separate, that your concern is in some way mine as well, that your suffering is my suffering. This transcends separation and the desire for survival.

This part of the Jesus story, with Satan and the temptations in the desert, can *seem* abstract and kind of fanciful, but if you look at what the underlying metaphors are trying to say, you'll find that it actually relates very much to daily life. There are many moments in any given week that life asks us: Where are you going to operate from? What's your intention? What do you really value? Do you value connectedness and deep truth, or do you value fear and survival? It's easy to say you value connectedness and truth, but when you're put in the situation where you feel uncertain, where you don't know the outcome, when acting from the deepest truth and love will cost you something, what are you going to do? What do you value the most? This is what Jesus is encountering here.

THE SECOND TEMPTATION

The second temptation has to do with hubris. I think we've all experienced hubris at times when we get a little too high on ourselves or think we're a little nobler than we actually are. Hubris in this sense can be unintentional, but in its darker aspect, hubris becomes real arrogance to the point of delusion.

In the Gospel of Matthew, Jesus' next temptation is described like this:

> Then the devil took him to the holy city and had him
> stand on the highest point of the temple. "If you are the
> Son of God," he said, "throw yourself down. For it is
> written: 'He will command his angels concerning you,
> and they will lift you up in their hands, so that you will
> not strike your foot against a stone.'" [Matthew 4:5–6, NIV]

What Satan is saying here is, "You're so great, look what you've realized. Now prove it to me; show off for me; be someone special for me; exercise this great enlightenment that you have." And Jesus answers him simply, "Do not put the Lord your God to the test." [Matthew 4:7, NIV] It's such a simple answer. It may seem antiquated, but what he's really saying is, "I won't show off. Even though I'm the Son of God, I'm not going to announce it. I'm not going to go out and *prove* it. I know, and that's enough. I will not be tempted to misuse my power." And as a human being, is it enough that *you* know, or do you always have to be acknowledged for what you know? Do you have to seek out attention? Do you have to show off? Or, if you attain great powers, will you be tempted into using them for self-serving purposes? Once again, what Jesus is showing us is what it looks like to align with our deeper truth. That's what is being conveyed: when tested, what do you align with?

Let me give two examples of how spiritual hubris might look. One is personal and one is more observational. The personal example occurred not too long after my first awakening, which happened when I was twenty-five years old. Some months after that awakening, I was at my teacher's house, where I went every week, meditating with other students. I remember as I was sitting there meditating, all of a sudden this sense of arrogance arose, and I found myself feeling very spiritually elevated compared to everyone else in the room. Even at the time it was horrific to me; these thoughts would go through my mind of how much better I was than the others because I'd had this realization and they hadn't.

This was hubris in the form of arrogance. It emerged from somewhere deep in the subconscious, and when it rose to the surface it shocked and horrified me. Luckily, as soon as it arose I saw it and *knew* it was ridiculous. I certainly didn't act on it. In fact, as I sat there I tried all sorts of things to get rid of it. First I just tried to resist it; I kept telling myself, "I know this isn't true, I know this isn't real, but why is this happening?"

And so the weeks went by, but each Sunday morning when I'd go visit my teacher and be with the other students, the same thing would happen as soon as I sat down. I even had a term for it inside of me; I called it "arrogant guy." I went through all of my strategies to get rid of arrogant guy. After resisting—which I knew wouldn't work anyway—I tried to accept it. Then I tried to lovingly, compassionately embrace the arrogance. I tried every trick in the book. After about two months of this recurring thought-stream of arrogance arising in my mind, I was once again with my teacher on a Sunday morning, sitting with the group of students, and once again as I was meditating arrogant guy arose. I finally just realized there's nothing I can do about it. I can't get rid of it through resistance; I can't get rid of it through loving it; I can't get rid of it through hating it; I can't get rid of it through understanding it. So in that moment I didn't try to do anything with it at all. I just saw it arise—no resistance, no indulgence, nothing. And when it arose in that space, where there was no relationship with it, all of a sudden it literally just popped like a bubble, and it was gone. And I have to tell you, I was really, really relieved. So I was lucky in that instance because I knew that it wasn't true. I knew it was arrogance and saw it for what it was, but still I had to go through it.

I've seen many people over lots of years have awakening experiences, and I've seen many ways that this hubris can display itself. In Zen we call this sort of hubris "drunk on emptiness." The word *emptiness* means something akin to the word *spirit*, so "drunk on emptiness" suggests a sort of exuberance for the awakened state itself. When the awakened state first appears, often it's so new and so unexpected that there's a certain kind of exaltation. It's simply part of the energy field of the awakened state, especially at the beginning, and it's very easy to get caught up in that exuberance, like having a new toy to play with. Most people who experience this spiritual hubris are not ill intentioned, but nonetheless we can begin to lose touch with the very human dimension of life. We can become full of ourselves and go around telling everybody that we know what's true. That's a very obvious form of arrogance.

Another form of this hubris occurs when we are so taken up into our exalted state that we stop paying attention to our relative life. There's a story that really highlights this, and it involves my teacher's teacher. Her teacher, a Zen master who had come over from Japan, was meeting with one of his senior students, who had a wife and several children. One day the teacher asked him, "So, how's your wife, how's the kids?"

The student said, "You know, it's not really going that well."

The teacher said, "So tell me what's going on."

"Well," the student said, "my wife says I'm not paying attention to her, and the kids say I'm not spending enough time with them."

And the teacher asked, "Well, are you?"

"Well, you know, since I had this big spiritual shift, my spiritual life is comparatively so much more vital," the student answered. "It seems like this is the reality, and my family life doesn't seem as compelling or real to me anymore."

There was a retreat coming up, and the teacher said, "I want both you and your wife to come on this next retreat."

Well, being a good student he agreed, and his wife agreed as well. And so they came to the retreat thinking that they would be sitting in meditation like you do at Zen retreats. Instead, the teacher called them both up and said, "I've set aside a room just for you. There's a bed in that room, and I want you both to spend the next twenty-four hours on that bed together. I don't care what you talk about, if you don't talk at all, if you're on opposite ends of the bed—I just want you to stay on that bed."

The next day they came back and the teacher said, "So, how's it going?"

"Well," the student said, "you know, after about ten hours on that bed we started to have a chat, and we began to relate a little bit more."

"Well, that's good," said the teacher. "Now, I want you to spend another twenty-four hours on that bed together." And so it went over the entire seven-day retreat; they literally spent seven days on a bed together. What happened over those seven days is that, when the student *had* to be with his wife and to confront what he was avoiding, eventually his own hubris started to break down. His sense of superiority; his sense that his wife and family couldn't understand him; his sense that they weren't as inherently valuable as the ultimate truth he realized—all of it started to break down over those seven days, and they started to talk and relate once again. It saved his marriage; it saved his relationship with his kids. In a sense it brought him back down to earth, not by pulling him out of what he realized, but by grounding the raw energy of the awakened state back into life and back into his family. He was very lucky that he *had* a family, because if you don't have something that can ground you, you can get really off balance at such times.

It's good to be reminded that hubris, left unchecked, can have serious consequences in our lives. If we don't notice soon enough, we might just realize too late that we've lost some very important things in our lives. The beauty of this story is that it reminds us: keep your feet firmly planted on the soil, keep your consciousness and your heart open, and stay available to this relative world and all the human beings within it.

THE THIRD TEMPTATION

The third temptation is all about power, and certainly our world has many examples of people who've been tempted by power. People are willing to sacrifice their morality, their sense of right and wrong, for money or power or influence. We see this on display in the political arena, where people will say almost anything to get a vote. They'll say one thing one week and the opposite thing the next week. On a personal level, each of us in our lives can see this temptation at work, in big ways or small. Where are we selling out for power and influence, to get ahead, to secure what our egos want? This desire for power is a perennial theme in the human story.

Now in the Jesus story, this temptation takes on a mythic form. In Matthew, during the third temptation it says: "Again, the devil took him to a very high mountain and showed him all the kingdoms of the world and their splendor. 'All this I will give you,' he said, 'if you bow down and worship me.'" [Matthew 4:8–9, NIV]

Satan is saying bow down and forsake the truth; forsake that still small voice within you that knows the correct orientation and give yourself to illusion. Do this, and you can have *everything*.

"Jesus said to him, 'Away from me, Satan! For it is written: worship the Lord your God and serve him only.'" [Matthew 4:10, NIV]

73

When this temptation for power arises, Jesus says, "Away from me. Sorry, forget it. I'm not buying it." Now remember, Satan is not *out there* in the world, but a personification of *internal* forces of darkness. Satan represents what in our modern vernacular we would call the inner shadow. Satan is that voice in the back of your mind—and maybe for some people right in the front—that says, "Get what you can, as fast as you can. Take advantage; that's what you really want to do."

The teaching here is about what it looks like to stay aligned—aligned with the vital force of the universe, aligned with your love, aligned with what you really know to be true. This alignment is different than simply doing the right thing. These are not ultimately moral or ethical questions, though they have moral and ethical consequences. But Jesus is engaged here on an entirely different level. This is someone who has had a deep spiritual shift; he's awakened to his true nature and he knows himself to be divine *being*. What trials and temptations might arise to one who has realized himself as divine *being?* You might think that all that shadow material would be dispelled and immediately disappear upon awakening—and much of it does. But awakening itself will scour the deep realms and shadow areas of the unconscious and bring it up into consciousness. Thus, it's very common that people who have had deep and significant spiritual awakenings will at some point have to meet their inner shadow at a very deep and fundamental level. Through dealing with this shadow material, we become more and more aligned—but not with ideas of right and wrong, good and bad. There is a different kind of alignment here, an alignment with that inner sense of spiritual reality, love, and divine *being*.

COMING INTO ALIGNMENT

Once Jesus has passed these tests, he comes back out of the wilderness. He's dealt with the deepest shadow material; he's met every weakness; he's found that, under pressure, he aligns himself with the deeper reality, no matter what. And this theme of aligning with the truth, aligning with the deeper spiritual reality of oneness, will be a theme that runs throughout the gospel stories, just as it's a theme that runs through all of our lives. Am I going to be truthful? Am I going to live from that reality? Am I going to be open right here and right now? These may seem like simple questions, but at any given moment—for example, when you're talking to someone and an argument or disagreement arises—it can be so easy to go into that reactive place of the mind that wants to be right, that demands to be understood or wants to win.

With what do we align ourselves at that moment? What do we value? What do we really want? At that moment, if we remain in alignment with our spiritual *being,* then we are connected to a deep state of quiet clarity and love, in which we have not disconnected from one another. As soon as you move out of truth, you *feel* it, kinesthetically; you feel it in your body when you've disconnected. Have you ever had a conversation in which you said something that wasn't entirely real or entirely true? At that moment, if you're sensitive, you feel an energetic severing of the cord of connection.

Correspondingly, when we move into the deep and intimate truth that arises from silence and stillness and love, then we feel a deep energetic connectivity, an intimacy with the moment and with whoever and whatever is in that moment. This is how even our physical bodies help us to align with spiritual reality, into the deeper dimensions of what's really true. When our bodies are suffering, when we feel internal conflict, then we know that we're not in balance. We're out of alignment with what is.

Again and again, the mythic elements of this story actually mirror the journey of spiritual awakening and also mirror the moment-to-moment realities of our lives. Don't go through life unconscious, the story is saying; these moments are happening for *you* also, in your daily life, if you would simply notice. You're being asked to align yourself to the deepest reality within you, to realize it and then to act from it.

FINDING THE RIGHT ORIENTATION

As soon as Jesus comes out of the desert, he begins to gather his disciples. Now, in the ancient world, a disciple would have been considered an initiate, somebody who is essentially an insider. This theme runs through the whole story—insiders and outsiders, initiates and non-initiates.

In the ancient world, each of the religions had a set of core stories, much like the story of Jesus. There were stories about the creation of the world, stories about the God-man, stories of exile and return. As happens today in many churches, the ordinary person was taught that these stories were essentially factual and historically accurate and true.

Now, an initiate was one who studied with a teacher until the teacher deemed that they were ready to delve deeper into the mystery of their own religious perspective. At a certain point the initiate would be told, "We told you that all these stories are historically accurate and historically true, but that viewpoint is really for the outsiders. That's all they can take and all they want to know; for them, it's good enough to have a story around with which to align their moral and ethical lives. But for you, for an initiate," the teacher would say, "we're going to peel back the veil; we're going to show you what this story is *really* all about."

And at that point, one of the first initiations would be to show the disciple that whatever the religious story might seem to be on the surface, it was actually a metaphor for the spiritual journey. It wasn't necessary to believe that the story was factual, because the story was conveying something more than fact and history. The story was conveying deep spiritual realities; it was meant as a mirror and a metaphor for what happens within you. Once you'd received this deeper meaning, then you'd be an initiate.

And this is Jesus' hope; this is his intention as he starts to gather his disciples. He gathers twelve disciples to whom he'll transmit the deepest reality of existence. He hopes to transmit to them what he calls the Kingdom of Heaven, what I call awakening to divine *being*. That's Jesus' mission. So he gathers his band of disciples around him. From this point on, the story becomes very fascinating as we see the development of Jesus' relationship with his disciples, as well as Jesus discovering his true role and destiny in the world.

Imagine that you've had a deep shift of consciousness. Imagine that you've suddenly realized that the person you thought you were your whole life wasn't really who you were, that the way you saw life wasn't really the way life was, that there was a transcendent reality upon which the whole world of forms and appearances rests and from which it derives its existence. You've had this whole identity of yourself and the way the world works, and then you have a spiritual awakening where the spirit descends into you, and you suddenly realize that your identity is not limited to the body, the mind, or the personality; rather there is a radiant spiritual reality within you.

Many people think this sounds wonderful, that such an awakening would add a sense of freedom and ease to life, which it does. But that's not actually what spiritual awakening is all about. Spiritual awakening is a profound *shift* of consciousness that upends your entire relationship to life. There is a big reorientation that takes place in the wake of such a titanic shift of consciousness. What do I do with my life? What's my role? What's my relationship with my friends, my family, my husband, my wife, my children? Your whole relationship with life starts to turn, and you don't initially know how you—as a human being—are going to fit into the picture. You don't know exactly what your role is going to be. Think of all the relationships in our lives and how we tend to orient ourselves around those relationships and the way we engage with them. Then, imagine you've had a profound shift of consciousness that calls all these relationships into question. How am I going to relate with people now? What am I going to talk with them about? What happens now that I see that so much of what I based my own personal life on was little more than a dream, a fantasy, something I thought was true but ended up not to be?

This is a profound realization and one that engenders a profound change of relationship with all of life. That doesn't just happen overnight. Throughout the Jesus story, we see Jesus discovering what his role is, how to teach, and what to teach. His first instinct is to do what was common at that time and place: to gather disciples, those who will become initiates, and try to transmit his teaching, to literally transmit his state of consciousness to them. That was the accepted method at that time.

As we'll see throughout the story, that doesn't necessarily work out very well for Jesus. The disciples, it turns out, don't really understand Jesus any better than anyone else in the story. Jesus is a very charismatic figure. People are drawn to him because he represents the spiritual reality, the radiance of divine *being;* when one has fully realized divine *being,* something about that person becomes compelling. Such a one is no longer primarily a person but a radiant presence. There's a type of charisma, different than the charisma of a celebrity or a public figure. It resonates deep in the hearts of human beings, because human beings resonate with one who shines with the divine reality. People are also terrified by it, because they don't know exactly what it is. They're drawn toward the radiance of awakened consciousness, but they also pull away because an awakened being is not predictable, and they don't operate the way we might expect.

Throughout the story, we'll see Jesus finding his role: gathering his disciples and trying to transmit his realization to them, becoming a healer and trying to teach through healing, telling parables and trying to teach through those parables. Late in his life, he begins to realize that his real teaching isn't healing, isn't to teach in parables, isn't even to transmit the deeper reality to his group of disciples, because that doesn't really work out. At some point he realizes that his real teaching is his life story. He himself is the teaching.

But all that will come later. For the moment he gathers together his small band of disciples, and he goes out to heal the sick and preach *repentance,* which means "to turn around, to have a change of heart."

THE HEALING MINISTRY

7

It is love alone that gives worth to all things.

ST. THERESA OF AVILA

Jesus begins his healings immediately after he has returned from his trials with Satan in the desert and gathered his first disciples. Many people assume that these healings have only to do with a kind of miraculous power Jesus has to heal physical ailments. But if we look more closely at how the story unfolds, we'll discover that almost every episode of healing has a deeper motive. Jesus' healings often occur within the broader context of repentance, which is his real concern, and also serve deeper metaphorical meanings regarding the restoration of divine *being* to its true place of sovereignty within oneself.

In other words, to Jesus, physical healing is secondary; there's almost always an underlying message that is ultimately more important to him than the healing itself.

THE LEPER

We find many subtle ways that Jesus is actually communicating a teaching as he's healing. The healings occur both on a physical and spiritual level and also serve as critiques of the society and religious leaders of his time. One of the first healings we encounter is that of Jesus healing a leper. In the ancient world, people were terrified of contracting leprosy, so to be a leper was to be ostracized, to be an extreme outsider. In the leper's story, found in both Mark and Matthew, the leper kneels before Jesus and asks Jesus to make him clean.

I find the leper's statement, "You can make me clean," really instructive. Imagine you've gone to someone to be healed of a physical ailment; I don't think the first thing you would ask of them is to make you clean. You would want them to heal you physically. When this leper says, "make me clean," it signifies that this healing—both from the standpoint of Jesus and of the leper—has to do with something deeper and more fundamental than physical healing. It also has to do with psychological and spiritual healing.

Jesus touches the man, and his leprosy immediately vanishes. Then Jesus sends the man away with a strong warning, telling him to go at once to the temple and undergo a purifying ritual and not to speak of his healing to anyone. Once again, I find the words and tone here very instructive. Jesus has undertaken a loving act, healing this man out of compassion, and the next thing he does is to sternly charge him to go through a ritual cleansing.

Of course, this warning ties in with the leper's first statement, "If you are willing, you can make me clean." This ritual doesn't necessarily have to do with a *physical* cleansing; it's a spiritual cleansing, a cleansing of his *being*, a reorientation of the heart. This signifies a very deep connection in the Gospels between spiritual impurity and physical ailment. Of course, today we know that there actually is a mind-body connection and understand that disease can be due to stress, anxiety, and emotional or psychological imbalance—all conditions that put great stress upon the body. So too in the ancient world: they understood as well that your inner psychological or spiritual state had a real connection to your physical state.

This doesn't mean that every illness we experience physically is caused by a psychological, emotional, or spiritual imbalance, but certainly some are, and this was known in the ancient world just as it is today.

Now the leper, as you can imagine, is so happy about being healed that he doesn't go to the temple as Jesus instructed; instead, he runs out and tells *everybody* what has happened. It's understandable, for he must have been absolutely amazed that he'd been healed. But again, there's a thread of deeper meaning. The leper from the beginning had an instinct that there was something unclean about him. When Jesus heals him and then commands him to go to the temple for ritual cleansing, we know there's some inner cause of the illness he's outwardly experiencing. But as soon as his health is restored and his energy has returned, he forgets all about his inner state.

This is a common reaction. In life we face very difficult circumstances sometimes—severe illness, divorce, job loss, anything that creates great psychological pressure—and at those times, we often become more available to inward transformation. When things go well, we can easily get lost in the outer aspects of life. When things don't go so well, that's often when human beings start to get introspective. We really start to look at ourselves, look at our motivations, and ask, "what is it that got me in this situation?" But often, as soon as we feel better, that kind of looking within is forgotten in our newfound exuberance.

This story of the leper's healing strikes me as a cautionary tale. We're not told what happens to the leper after that, but we know he didn't do what Jesus asked him to do, and he did do what Jesus asked him not to do. It leaves me wondering if at some point he'll get his leprosy back—because he didn't go through the ritual cleansing, because he forgot about his inner life in his exuberance about his healing. I think the potency and power of this story is in the way it connects with a very human tendency to become less conscious as we become more comfortable.

SPIRITUAL POWERS

It's interesting that in many of the healing stories Jesus says, "Don't tell anybody what has happened." He's keeping his real role in the world something of a secret; he doesn't want people to know his own destiny quite yet. I think he also is telling people not to tell others because each time someone does tell others, hordes of people come to him. People are attracted to powerful healers and miracle workers, and Jesus really didn't want the attention.

There were two reasons for this, I think. The first, as I mentioned, had to do with concealing his destiny, which we'll look at later. The other was simply that he didn't want to be surrounded by a lot of crowds demanding healing. My sense is that he saw inner spiritual transformation as the gift he was bringing to the world and didn't really want to be known as a healer. Healing was simply a means to an end, a means to bring about inner transformation. If the focus of his ministry were simply healing, few of his followers would likely be interested in the kind of deep and profound inner transformation that Jesus really intended to convey. Nonetheless, if you're a really powerful healer, you're going to attract crowds; it just goes with the territory.

The healings point to something else as well. As we awaken, as we enter into what you might call a higher state of consciousness, at some point it's very common to take on certain powers. In some traditions these spiritual powers are known as *siddhis* and can include powers of clairvoyance, powers of healing, and the power to foretell the future.

We think of the normal egoic state of consciousness, ordinary waking consciousness, as a natural state, simply because most people are in that state. But actually, this normal state of consciousness from which most people operate is extraordinarily limited, and it literally filters out or blocks out an immense dimension of *being* comprised of more subtle planes of consciousness. These abilities may come to us as we open to this wider consciousness. This doesn't mean that everybody who awakens gets powers of healing and clairvoyance or the ability to foretell the future; some people do and some people don't.

Power is a very dangerous aphrodisiac to the ego; many people are deeply attracted to power. Even in our ordinary everyday world, issues of power arise. If you lead a company or you're a manager, you're exercising power over people's lives; they have to fit in with the structure and power dynamics that were put in place by the people above them. Power at any level, whether its an intrinsic power or a relative power due to your position in the world, can really bring to light and activate desire, because power begets the desire for more power.

In every esoteric spiritual tradition there are grave warnings about indulging in these kinds of powers and seeking out the psychic abilities that may come with awakening. The usual counsel is neither to push away or deny these powers, nor to grasp or desire or indulge in them. In Jesus' case, what we get through the story is a vital reflection of what it means to use power wisely. Jesus is a man of great authority, great inner power, and great charisma, and people are deeply attracted to him, whether for healing or spiritual transformation or simply to be in his presence. In example after example, he wields this power with wisdom and love. Throughout the Gospels we see how Jesus utilizes power, when he utilizes it and when he pulls back and leaves things as they are. He's a master of the wise use of power.

MISSING THE MARK

Another of the healing stories, one that I find fascinating, is the story of the paralytic. A few days after he healed the leper, a paralyzed man is brought to Jesus for healing. All Jesus says to him is, "Son, your sins are forgiven." [Mark 2:5, NIV, ESV] And with that simple statement, "your sins are forgiven," the man is healed.

This brings up the whole question of the meaning of sin. The theme of sin is woven throughout the New Testament, often twined with forgiveness. Now, we've come to understand sin as a kind of moral failing, but that interpretation actually comes from the power structures of the church and religious authorities. If you can convince somebody that they are inherently impure and that there is a mistake at the center of their *being*, then sin becomes a wrongdoing that deserves blame.

Of course, there are times when we human beings have our moral failings and we don't live up to the dictates of the heart. But this interpretation doesn't really get to the original, more nuanced meanings of the word *sin*. In the original Greek, one of the meanings of *sin [hamartia]* is simply "to miss the mark." Now, imagine you've gone to confession, and the priest says to you, "Confess your sins." Imagine that this priest even accuses you of being a sinner; imagine how that would feel in your mind and heart, to be considered a moral failure. Now imagine instead how you'd feel if that priest were to say, "So, tell me, how have you missed the mark in your life?" There's an enormous difference in how these two interpretations of sin are held in our hearts, in our minds, in our bodies. If we understand that sin means to miss the mark, it's not so personal and damning.

Another meaning of sin is simply a flaw, like the flaw in a diamond. Well, every human being walking the earth has a flaw of one kind or another. There is no single, sanitized version of perfection that we all must measure up to. In this story, you'll notice Jesus isn't condemning the paralytic for his sins; he's not telling him he's a failure because of his sins; he's saying, "Your sins are forgiven."

This paralytic didn't even do anything to deserve that his sins be forgiven; he was simply carried and placed in the presence of Jesus. And this is really Jesus' greatest healing power, the power of his presence. This is true for each of us. The power of presence is a very potent healing force, not only for others but also within ourselves. And so, when Jesus says, "your sins are forgiven," he's saying, "I forgive you for all the ways that you've missed the mark." Jesus bestows his forgiveness upon people as a kind of healing balm. For a human being to receive true forgiveness is a potent thing. When the forgiveness is authentic, it has a very deep and powerful effect. Sometimes another forgives us, and sometimes we are called to forgive ourselves so that we can move on in a really heartful way. When we repent (have a change of heart), our sin (missing the mark) is forgiven. Then we are realigned with the wisdom of the unified heart.

So you see how these themes of sin and forgiveness are really linked together. They tell us that to miss the mark is not a terrible thing, that even to have a flaw—a flaw in our character perhaps—is not inherently evil. The healing balm is forgiveness; that's what heals the flaw. That's what allows us to rebalance ourselves, to find our inner equilibrium—psychic, emotional, and spiritual. That is really what Jesus does: he is righting the person, helping them to quickly find internal balance. When they find balance, when their inner state is unified, the healing takes place.

Of course this comes off as extraordinary in the Jesus story. It's a story after all, and it contains an ancient mythological motif about healing and what it signifies. When we read of extraordinary things like Jesus' ability to heal, we can be carried away by the outward forms of healing, amazed by this person Jesus' capacities and abilities. But metaphorically, what these healing stories point to is an inner healing: a coming into rightness, reorienting ourselves to divine *being* inside.

When this occurs, we're not lost in the egoic mind, not lost in desire, not lost in resistance. We have been righted; we have found that center point around which the world revolves. That center point is the Kingdom of Heaven—the place where everything is eternally and always ok. In that place, you feel nothing has ever gone wrong. In your externalized self—in the ego, the personality structure, even in your physical body—it can certainly feel like things have gone wrong. But when we reorient ourselves toward divine *being,* we discover a place inside of ourselves that the relative world of time never touches. It can't be defiled, it can't be wounded, it's eternally and always ok. In fact, it's more than ok—it's radiantly happy. These healing stories are a way of bringing attention back to that place, of reorienting the human heart, reorienting our minds, reorienting our spiritual perception.

THE POWER OF FORGIVENESS

Forgiveness is such an important part of Jesus' teaching. Forgiveness is a very potent force, not only in the Jesus story but also in the Christian theology that has developed in the two thousand years since, in which Jesus as Savior atones for the sins of all humankind through his death and resurrection. Thus, one of Jesus' key roles is to forgive.

Forgiveness comes from a deep openhearted state of compassion. Really, it comes from our spiritual essence—which I call divine *being*—because from our spiritual essence there is an understanding of what suffering is really all about. From the heart of divine *being*, what we realize is that everything that causes us pain and sorrow is ultimately born from misunderstanding. It's a type of illusion. Later in the story, at the crucifixion, when Jesus says, "Father, forgive them for they know not what they do," [Luke 23:34, ESV] this is what he's pointing to. When people are in a state of spiritual clarity—an inner state of psychological, emotional, and spiritual unity—then by the very nature of that unity, they don't act out of ignorance. Ignorance is simply a misunderstanding of the fundamental reality, of what we truly are.

When we lose the consciousness of our deepest self, our deepest *being* as divine *being* itself, then in a sense we go unconscious. Part of us goes to sleep, you might say. Then, we are prone to illusion. We misunderstand things. We think if someone insults us, for example, that we need to respond with anger; we forget that they're just expressing their own inner conflict, their own inner division, which is ultimately based on misunderstanding. The very root of sin, to use Jesus' language, is something that can be forgiven. It's forgivable because it's an unconscious act, a result of being spiritually asleep. We can't be blamed for being unconscious, for acting out our unconsciousness, even for feeling the effects of our unconsciousness within our psychology.

Everyone has those days when you feel like you've woken up on the good side of the universe, when everything just naturally feels whole and complete, when you're happy and at peace and you don't really know why. When this happens you're more aligned with life, and you naturally go about the day as a much more open person. You're more compassionate, and you're more loving, because compassion and love are expressions of being internally united. So forgiveness is ultimately an act that comes from that inner unification. One doesn't have to be entirely unified inwardly to forgive. Forgiveness can also come out of the sense of open-heartedness, of understanding that nobody is perfect.

The open heart is compassionate because it maintains an essential connection. But as soon as we separate ourselves from another—as soon as we say, "No, there's nothing in you that corresponds with something in me," as soon as we forget that you and I essentially share the same spiritual essence—then we cut ourselves off, and we go into blame. Forgiveness comes from that deep intuition of our sameness, of our shared humanity. That perception starts to lower the walls of defense, and being judgmental is ultimately a defensive game, a way of saying, "I am not like you." To forgive is really a way of saying, "I see something in you that's the same as in me." Then, even though you may be upset, even though the other person may have caused you pain or harm, when you connect with your shared humanity, there's forgiveness.

Forgiveness is probably the greatest healer there is. When we forgive someone, what we've forgiven we're no longer attached to, no longer controlled by. We can call it compassion, as they do in Buddhism. We can call it *agape*—selfless, universal love. Universal love was one of Martin Luther King Jr.'s central messages during the civil rights movement. His message was a message of peace, which is a kind of forgiveness. He wanted people of color to have the same rights and liberties as everyone else in America, but he wasn't dividing himself against anyone. He stood for the rights of all people, the dignity of all people, and didn't get caught in blame. He preached constantly against violence, because in his heart he had the capacity first to understand others and then to connect, even with those with whom he disagreed. I'm not saying that he connected in an intellectual sense, but rather in an essential sense; somewhere inside him was this sense of connection, and out of that came his capacity to forgive.

In the story of Jesus, the ultimate act of forgiveness comes near the end, when Jesus says from the cross, "Father, forgive them, for they know not what they do." [Luke 23:34, ESV] Now, if you can forgive someone for torturing you and hanging you on a cross, you can forgive anything. And why forgive? Because *they know not what they do.* This forgiveness comes from a deep spiritual understanding of the causes of suffering—and also of those who inflict suffering, for those who inflict suffering have always had suffering inflicted upon them at some prior time. When we start to realize this, our heart opens. I'm sure you've seen images of the sacred heart of Jesus—that big red heart in the middle of Jesus' chest radiating forgiveness to all of humanity. It's one of the most potent symbols of the whole Christian spiritual tradition. It's Jesus' greatest gift, the most powerful healing balm that exists.

DESTROYING ALL BOUNDARIES

Now, when Jesus heals the paralytic by forgiving his sins, he upsets the Pharisees, who can be seen as the religious fundamentalists or radicals of the time. The reason they're so angry is that, from their viewpoint, God is the only one who has the capacity to forgive sins. The religious institutions that Jesus was born into, and often found himself surrounded by, were very threatened by his presence. In their minds, his actions were the ultimate sin. Jesus was forgiving sins, healing people, and attracting great crowds. All these were real threats to the religious powers of the day. This theme of relationship to power appears in many of Jesus' healings, because the religious hierarchy is very unsettled by the presence of Jesus. In a certain sense, their power has been usurped by a greater power. In Jesus, the power of spirit itself has awakened; it's a constant reminder to these religious institutions that their hierarchical power pales in comparison to the power of divine *being* that Jesus is and that he represents in these stories. The power structures are upset by Jesus' power, and we see this theme arise again and again throughout the Gospels.

There's another encounter between Jesus and the Pharisees in which Jesus and his disciples are dining at Levi's house. The Gospel of Mark reads, "While Jesus was having dinner at Levi's house, many tax collectors and sinners were eating with him and his disciples, for there were many who followed him." [Mark 2:15, NIV] These sinners are people of ill repute, on the lowest rungs of society, and tax collectors were even less popular in the ancient world than they are now. In the ancient world, taxation was a very personal transaction, because a tax collector could demand money from you right on the spot.

For Jesus, a spiritual figure of great magnitude, to be sitting down with the lowest rungs of society was simply not acceptable at that time. In the ancient world there was a very clear stratification of society, similar to Indian society with the Brahmins at the top and the untouchables at the lowest rung. There were clear boundaries around whom you could associate with and whom you couldn't, between who was clean and pure and who was unclean and impure. Jesus crossed all of those boundary lines, destroying them at almost every turn. In the eyes of the Pharisees, Jesus has done something terrible, a high spiritual figure dining with the lowest classes. People in positions of power are on the highest rungs of society. In order to keep their high status, in order to be seen as mighty and noble, they *need* to have people that are seen as lesser. From a religious point of view, these distinctions mattered deeply, but to Jesus they didn't matter at all. Jesus destroys the boundaries that separate people because that's what spirit does: it sees the unity of all beings. It sees what we all share in common instead of what separates us and divides us.

Another of the healing stories begins when Jesus enters the temple. There he encounters a man with a shriveled hand. The religious authorities are watching him to see if he would dare to heal the man on the Sabbath. Jesus knows what the authorities are thinking, and he asks the crippled man to stand. "He looked around at them in anger and, deeply distressed at their stubborn hearts, said to the man, 'Stretch out your hand.' He stretched it out, and his hand was completely restored. Then the Pharisees went out and began to plot with the Herodians how they might kill Jesus." [Mark 3:5–6, NIV]

This is a real turning point in the Jesus story. Jesus has gone into the temple, and his mere presence is antagonistic to those in power. He's noticed the Pharisees watching him and whispering, looking down at him. This is a very human emotion he's experiencing; he notices what's going on around him and becomes outraged. He's angry because he can feel the divisions within them, the hierarchies of religious authority, and he's put off by all the divisions that human beings create. So he acts very abruptly, even sternly, saying to the man with the withered hand, "Stretch out your hand." The man stretches out his hand and—*boom*—he's healed right on the spot.

This story has less to do with healing than with Jesus breaking the boundary lines of the religious power structure.

It's telling us something very important about spirit, our true divine *being*. We tend to live in a state where our *true being*, our true sovereignty, our true power is hidden away inside. It's tucked deep in the shadowy corners of our unconscious, so that the egoic mind—with its wants and its desires and its love of power and even its love of being a victim of life—can have full rein. But when spirit begins to awaken within you, you *feel* that it is a force that is uncontainable. This is often when people begin to pull back. They're seeking enlightenment, seeking God, seeking the ultimate nature of reality, but when they begin to touch upon it, it's not what they expect it to be. It's a force of great inner vitality, untamed and untamable: it breaks through all of the mind's structures that perpetuate separation.

This theme of breaking through all structures of ignorance and separation is the driving force of Jesus' life. Now, Jesus doesn't break through structures just to break through them; he has no inherent problem with authority; it's only the corruption of power that angers him. He's not fighting against power and authority per se. Jesus himself is an extraordinarily powerful being, and he operates with great inner authority. His life is a life of spirit, and spirit breaks down the false power structures—first in your own mind and then in the outside world. In the Gospels, spirit is a dynamic and unpredictable source of vitality and liberation.

Many of the societal and religious rules keep the human heart contained, and as a result, most human beings feel boxed in. Unfortunately, when we turn to religion, often the churches box us in even more. They tell us that we are inherently flawed, that we need to be forgiven for this sin, this stain that we carry. The first and most important function of religion is to connect you with the mystery of life and the mystery of your own *being*.

When religion fails to do this, it has betrayed its primary mission, and all we are left with is dogma and belief.

The churches, synagogues, and temples of *all* religions are entrusted with this—to interpret the old stories and teachings so they open us to the transcendent mystery of life, not so they confine us in the egoic state through fear, guilt, and repression. In my teaching work I constantly meet people who were brought up in the church, but at some point turned away from their religion because they were tired of hearing over and over again that their fundamental nature was flawed, that simply to be born was some sort of cosmic mistake in which they were forever burdened with the stain of sin. Many people receive this sort of message from their childhood religion and at some point reject it because it's so painful and, most importantly, because it doesn't correspond with inner intuition.

One of the reasons I think it's so powerful to renew our understanding of the Jesus story is because it's the foundational story of Western culture, and it dominates so much of our lives— even if we don't think of ourselves as Christian at all. There are beautiful things about the Christian message, about Jesus' message, and about the presence that Jesus represents, but often it doesn't come through in the churches we attend. Jesus' message was about intimate, personal, immediate access to divine *being*, to the Kingdom of Heaven within. That's what he preached. For him there was no intermediary. No priest was necessary to connect you with the mystery of God, only an open heart and an open mind. This viewpoint got him in a lot of trouble with the religious authorities of his time, because power structures almost always claim to be a necessary intermediary between you and the divine. In Jesus' time, just as today, many religious institutions fail to fulfill their primary directive, which is to connect us with our spiritual nature.

TRUST IN THINGS UNSEEN

Soon after healing the man with the withered hand, Jesus is followed by a large crowd who press in around him. People are intrigued by this charismatic, spiritually charged being. Word is spreading fast, and more and more people are coming to listen to him and to be with him. Now, as he's walking through a crowd, a woman who has suffered from bleeding for twelve years reaches out and touches his garment. "Immediately her bleeding stopped and she felt in her body that she was freed from her suffering." [Mark 5:29, NIV]

Jesus immediately realizes what has happened, and he turns to the crowd and asks, "Who touched my clothes?" Finally the woman comes forward, fearfully, and kneels at his feet. And Jesus says to her: "Daughter, your faith has healed you. Go in peace and be freed from your suffering." [Mark 5:34, NIV] This story brings out another important truth about healing. Jesus doesn't say, "I have healed you, daughter, now go in peace." He says, "Your *faith* has made you well, now go in peace." It's not the power of Jesus that heals people. In fact, Jesus says over and over again that he's doing the work of the Father, that he's a conduit through which the healing presence moves and functions. And so Jesus is always very clear that his human self does not contain all the power, that the human self is not the healer, that the human self is not the powerful charismatic being. He attributes all those powers to the realm of spirit, to the Kingdom of God.

What heals the woman is her faith, her trust in things unseen. Usually we think of faith simply as something we *believe in* in the absence of proof. In the modern day, faith is almost always associated with some sort of belief structure. But Jesus never defines what someone must have faith *in;* he doesn't say "your faith in me has healed you." Rather, it's faith itself, the trust in things unseen that heals.

So what does it mean to trust in something you can't see? We can't see the majority of life's structures: we can't see the atoms or the electrons, or the vast emptiness that comprises any physical object with the naked eye. All objects are more *nothing* than *something*. In other words, there's more space within them than there is physical substance. And yet, when we look at a chair or our face in the mirror, what we see is the form. We don't see that within the form there is actually more emptiness, more of the unseen than the seen.

We can't see gravity either, but we experience gravity every moment of our lives. Without it we'd all just float away. Love is a very real experience, central to human existence. We come in to existence by love, we are sustained through life by love, and hopefully when we die, we die *into* love, we surrender into love. But what is love? You can't see it, you can't weigh it, it has no color, and yet it's a very, very real thing. And so, when Jesus talks about faith he's alluding to the power to trust in something you can't see or even comprehend with the dualistic mind. And yet faith can open you to an order of reality far beyond ordinary perception. That reality is what Jesus called the Kingdom of Heaven, what in other traditions is called enlightenment. And enlightenment cannot be grasped with your mind; it can only be awoken to. It is a complete change of perception from ordinary egoic consciousness to the consciousness of unity and completeness. This is what faith can open you up to, if you have faith in the still point within yourself. Find that place within yourself where nothing ever moves, and through that you can gain entrance into the Kingdom.

When people are in despair or great suffering, those are the moments when human beings start to open up to other possibilities. It's as if suffering stretches our capacity to consider that there are other energies in life—things that we can't see, that we haven't learned about, but that we might reach out to. There's an old saying, "there are no atheists in a fox hole." When your life is on the line, you naturally reach out to a higher divinity.

Now, some may argue that when you're frightened, you make things up to help you through that difficult time, and perhaps there's some truth to that. But in my experience, both in my own life and in what I've been told by many people over the years, when we suffer it does open us in some way. When life is going well, the egoic mind thinks it's in control and it's got this whole thing figured out. People tend not to look into the deeper mystery of their existence when everything is going well. But when life isn't going so well—when we're in a place of strain, of anxiety, of sorrow—that's when people start to consider other possibilities.

In the Zen Buddhist tradition that I come from, a great emphasis is placed on meditation. It took me a long time to realize that to meditate, to sit there in silence is actually an act of great faith. To sit in silence is to let go of the dualistic mind, of the ego that believes, "I must be in control of my spiritual life. I must be leading it in order for anything to happen." But when we sit in silence and stillness, we're letting go of that. To meditate is an act of faith; it is the highest form of prayer. It's the silent prayer in which we open up to the divine mystery of our own existence. That's really the essence of meditation.

Often when people meditate, they're trying very hard to control their minds, to keep certain thoughts from appearing. This act shows they have no faith at all; their meditation is a completely ego-driven activity. I'm not saying such activity has no part to play, no usefulness, but ultimately to connect us with the mystery of *being*, an act of faith is required. To have faith is to let go of control; it's to release the ego's instinct to always be in charge. So faith opens up that aspect of the ego that wants to control everything and think that it has all the answers. This is what faith is: an opening of the heart, an opening of the mind. Jesus knew from his own experience that when you open your heart and mind, you literally open yourself to the healing presence. You open yourself to that which can transform you, physically, spiritually, and psychologically.

To be open *is* the act of faith. This is extraordinarily important in all of the healing stories of Jesus. In fact, I find it interesting in these stories that people come to Jesus in order to be healed, but when they see him, they also understand something about his true nature. As we go through the story, we'll see that often his own disciples are really quite baffled by him; they're attracted to him, but they don't really understand who and what he is. Of course, the religious hierarchy is threatened by him and doesn't know what to make of him either.

The Gospels show Jesus as a man who is very much alone—probably one of the most alone human beings who ever walked the earth. Why? Because throughout his entire life almost no one really and truly understood him, understood the significance of who he was and what he was doing. Yet the people who did have an intuition about who and what he was were those who sought healing. It's as if their suffering opened them and allowed them to see something about him that many others didn't see. And so I think this is another example of the way that suffering can stretch us—stretch our hearts, but also stretch our perception. When our perception opens, we can intuit things that we couldn't intuit before. The sick and the needy have a way of intuiting who Jesus really is. In a number of examples, they receive not only a physical healing but a deep spiritual healing as well.

MY NAME IS LEGION

8

> Jesus said, "Let him who seeks continue seeking
> until he finds. When he finds, he will become
> troubled. When he becomes troubled, he will
> be astonished, and he will rule over all."
>
> **GOSPEL OF THOMAS**

The next healing story I want to examine is the healing of Legion. Legion doesn't have a physical illness. He's not a paralytic; he's not blind; he's not bleeding; his hand isn't withered. Legion's illness is of the mind, of the psyche. In modern vernacular, we'd probably just call him insane.

POSSESSED BY DEMONS

Legion, when Jesus meets him, is clearly mad. No one can control him, and he cannot control himself. The Gospel of Mark calls him "a man with an impure spirit," and often he's heard screaming late at night. "This man lived in the tombs, and no one could bind him anymore, not even with a chain." [Mark 5:3,

NIV] This is someone unbalanced and unrestrained, someone profoundly unstable mentally and emotionally. He is literally out of control. No one else can control him and he cannot control himself. Jesus asks his name, and he answers, "My name is Legion, for we are many." [Mark 5:9, ESV]

This is one of my favorite lines in the entire Jesus story. When Legions says, "My name is Legion, for we are many," what's speaking to Jesus is not Legion the man. Legion the person—the sane, rational human being—has been completely usurped by something else, by "the many," as Legion says. Now, when Legion says, "for we are many," what are the many? Our modern interpretation would be that Legion has a completely fractured psyche. When the psyche fractures, it's like a pane of glass dropped on the ground; it shatters into many bits and pieces. Someone to whom this has happened is literally lost in the unconscious; that becomes their reality. When you walk by a street corner and someone is mumbling to himself or shouting to people who aren't there, you know that they have been overcome by the unseen realms of their unconscious. For someone who's had a psychotic break, the unconscious *is* reality, as chaotic and unpredictable as it may be.

Now in Jesus' day, the explanation for the "many" of Legion isn't a fractured psyche, but demons. So in the story, when Legion says, "we are many," it's the demons that are talking to Jesus. Demons represent the fractured mind, in which many selves are in conflict. It's a more extreme version of the normal egoic state, which I remember one Buddhist teacher describing as, "The normal amount of hate, ignorance, and greed." Even in the normal state of egoic consciousness, in most human beings there are many selves, not one self. One day you feel like you're a good person, the next day you don't feel like you're good. One hour you feel worthy, the next hour something happens, and you feel unworthy. One minute you feel very competent, full of energy and confidence; the next minute you feel incompetent and downtrodden. So this quickly changing inner sense of who we are is another lens for looking at "the many." The egoic state of consciousness itself is a fractured state made up of multiple personas. It's a state in which many psychological forces are at odds with each other. This creates psychological friction, and our name for psychological friction is suffering.

In the modern day, we can debate whether there are demons or not. We can interpret demons through a modern psychological lens, as shards of a fractured psyche. Either way, the experience they point to is something real. In my seventeen years of teaching, there are many times when I'm talking with someone and, at a certain point, there's a very clear, literal perception of something completely taking them over. I've seen it occur right in the middle of a sentence, when suddenly they just completely disappear and something else comes in. What takes over is often very dark, even malicious. It enjoys the suffering—either its own suffering or that which it inflicts on others. Whether we want to think of this as a demon, as a dark entity or energy field, or as inner psychological forces in the unconscious, I don't think it really matters.

THE PAIN-BODY

The contemporary spiritual teacher Eckhart Tolle talks about what he calls "the pain-body." The pain-body is an energy field filled with negativity. We go into the pain-body when we have a conditioned response to a situation—for example, we feel insulted in a conversation, or something said to us evokes a painful memory. To call it "the pain-body" is a perfect description because as soon as you are *moved* into it by your conditioning, you feel an internal conflict.

If you're sensitive, if your perception is open, you can feel when someone moves into the pain-body, even if they aren't saying anything. I can walk into a room and know instantly if someone's pain-body has been activated. People are thrown into it because of how they are programmed inside to react to various circumstances. You could also see demons as the pain-body; if the pain-body gets really intense, it takes over consciousness, and you are totally lost.

So, Legion is many, and he is completely lost. His humanity has been taken over by the darker forces. Now, one of Jesus' great healing powers is the ability to cast out demons—in other words, to cast out pain, suffering, and darkness. When Jesus addresses Legion's demons, "Come out of this man, you impure spirit!" [Mark 5:8, NIV] the demons beg him not to simply cast them out. They don't want to be annihilated. Instead, seeing a large herd of pigs nearby, the demons beg Jesus, "Send us among the pigs; allow us to go into them." [Mark 5:12, NIV] It's a very bizarre twist to the story. So Jesus gives the demons permission to enter this herd of pigs, about two thousand in number. As soon as the pigs are infested with these demons—with the pain-body, with suffering—they rush off a cliff into the sea and drown.

Now, this is very dramatic, but remember that each element of the story is made larger than life because it's trying to represent something inside our experience so obvious that we can't miss it. Here it represents our own inner demons, not necessarily as entities, but simply as the shadow side of certain energies. Joseph Campbell, the great scholar of myth, wrote, "Gods suppressed become devils, and often it is these devils whom we first encounter when we turn inward." When you unleash a powerful force within you, when you return it to its true nature or original form, as we might say in Buddhism, then it has the power of a God. But that same force, when you deny it or push it down into your unconscious, becomes something dark and shadowy. It becomes a demon—and everyone has their demons.

WRATH AND LOVE

I used to hold retreats in a wonderful Tibetan Buddhist temple, and inside the meditation room, the walls were covered with thangkas. Thangkas are paintings on silk depicting all different kinds of deities, and these deities are actually representations of psychological, emotional, and spiritual forces within *you*. So imagine this meditation hall full of thangkas showing dozens of different deities, some of them quite graphic. There are wrathful deities with blood dripping off their teeth, skulls in their hands, or a bloodied sword they've just used to lop somebody's head off. And there are also deities who are quite heavenly and beautiful, healing deities who are soft and open and available. From demonic to beatific and everything in between, the whole array of human experience and emotion can be found among these deities.

In Tibet, these thangkas are used as objects of contemplation. Traditionally, you might use the image of a particular deity as an object of meditation, and by doing this you're evoking what that artistic representation symbolizes within you. So if you're meditating on a wrathful deity of great energy and you meditate on it very deeply, it will start to evoke that reality, that energy within you. It may be an energy that makes you very uncomfortable. It may bring up unresolved issues in your life—issues that have to do with that particular inner energy field, that psychological and spiritual force evoked through the contemplation of the deity. This can be a very powerful practice, because it scours the depths of the unconscious, and in doing so it brings to light the very best in you, the saintly, heavenly aspect of your nature, and also the darkest, most horrific parts of your nature. Because it's only when we can see all of ourselves—the light and the shadow; the good, bad, and indifferent—that we can embody these energies so they're no longer frightening and in possession of us.

When you really become the inner state of consciousness that a deity represents, then even a wrathful deity may be experienced as a very pure and vivid kind of energy. When you look long enough at one face of a psychological force, eventually it will turn and reveal its other face, like heads and tails of the same coin. So even a very wrathful energy, when you embody it without fear, can be experienced very purely, immediately and intimately. Then you begin to realize that within that wrathfulness is a great clarity of peace and love.

Of course, in the Jesus story there are many examples of Jesus being wrathful, but his wrath comes from a place not only of clarity, but also of love and compassion. For example, on several occasions he becomes upset with the religious hierarchy for the way that they close down people's access to the transcendent mystery. He's angry because he loves what's in all human beings. He knows there's something beautiful and powerful and liberating within every being and within the structure of reality itself, and he's upset because sometimes even our greatest religious institutions, if they're not careful, can begin to represent the world instead of the ultimate reality. In other words, religions start representing *themselves,* the continuation of the structure, the continuation of the hierarchy and wealth and power, and then they actually block us off from the transcendent mystery that they're entrusted to help awaken in us. So Jesus' wrath is actually tied to his love for humanity and his compassion for its suffering; anything that perpetuates that suffering becomes the object of his wrath.

As I've said, Jesus is a man of *action*. This is why he's such a powerful figure in today's spirituality. Today, the majority of people who have had authentic, deep spiritual callings aren't necessarily called to leave the world and join the monastery or disappear into a cave. The spiritual impulse today is not generally an impulse toward renouncing the world. Sometimes it will still work that way, and it's a perfectly legitimate way for spirit to manifest itself, but more and more I see a different spiritual calling—not to renounce the world, but to transform the world from the heart of spirit. I think that's where the story of Jesus becomes very relevant and very powerful, because Jesus himself was a man of action, a man of the world, even as he was a living presence of what lies beyond the world of forms.

Jesus isn't like the Buddha in this respect. He wasn't drawn to create a monastic movement within a new tradition like the Buddha did. Jesus isn't interested in form or structure *at all;* he breaks apart almost *any* form he encounters. In fact in the Gospel of Thomas there is a verse that reads: "Jesus said, 'Men think, perhaps, that it is peace which I have come to cast upon the world. They do not know that it is dissension which I have come to cast upon the earth: fire, sword, and war.'" [Gospel of Thomas 16]

This might seem opposed to the openhearted, loving presence of Jesus most of us imagine. Of course, love and compassion are a powerful part of what Jesus represents, but he also represents the dynamic force of spirit engaged in the world, and I think we need more examples of what engaged spirituality actually looks like. Now, who knows how much or how little this narrative may have been embellished over time to make a compelling and powerful story. As always, we're meant to read this story mythically and metaphorically, not as something confined to fact and history. To think that you need to go out into the world and act as Jesus acts in the story would be to misread it, to take it too literally. But if you read the story metaphorically, you can start to get a feel for this more engaged spirituality, what could be called "spirituality in action."

REORIENTED TOWARD DIVINE *BEING*

When Jesus heals Legion, he actually tells Legion to go share his story—just the opposite of what he said earlier to the leper. As I often say to people, the movement of spirit isn't really consistent; it moves in a way that feels appropriate and on the mark at the time. If to sin is to miss the mark, then not to sin is to be on the mark. To be on the mark means to know what is needed and true and relevant right here and right now, so of course one has to stay very awake, very present, and very open to what's required in the present moment.

When the demons are cast from him, Legion is transformed. He's sitting there in total peace and total well-being; he's no longer missing the mark. He's no longer many; he's now one. This is an example not of a physical healing, but of a psychological and spiritual healing. When Jesus took those forces of conflict out of Legion, then Legion's whole being naturally oriented itself around the oneness of divine *being*. The image of Legion, sitting perfectly calm, perfectly composed, tells us he has become one.

Now, my sense is that Jesus told Legion to go out and tell people what happened because Legion received a healing that was not just physical. Legion received a very deep spiritual healing. In a certain sense, Legion was rendered enlightened, and that's what Jesus wants to convey. That's what his mission is all about— waking you up to divine *being* inside yourself. Legion has had an inner spiritual revolution, an instantaneous righting of his being. As I have already said, there's always a spiritual component when Jesus heals someone, but as we saw earlier, when the leper was healed, he ran off and told everyone what had happened, and didn't go to the temple for purification. That's an indication that his inner being wasn't completely righted; otherwise, he would have followed through with what Jesus asked of him. On the other hand, when Jesus is getting into his boat to leave, Legion begs to come with him. But Jesus says, "That's not for you; go out into the world and tell your story." You see, Legion is completely righted. Legion is rendered enlightened; he doesn't need to follow Jesus, and Jesus knows that. He doesn't need to follow Jesus because he understands what Jesus is all about.

There are many other healing stories in the Gospels, but I just wanted to share a few of them that I think portray the deeper themes of Jesus' healing ministry. As I read it, the whole healing ministry was really Jesus' first form of teaching. Later in the story he starts to move away from the medium of healing, and you can understand why: once you're known as a healer, everybody wants to be healed. Wherever Jesus goes, people crowd around him. At times in his story, he's trying to get away from the crowds and have a little solitude.

Jesus didn't care about this kind of adulation. He chose twelve disciples and never more than twelve. He wasn't interested in numbers; he was interested in inner transformation. At some point his healing ministry actually started to get in the way of his teaching because people were coming to him for the wrong reasons. They were coming to him as a spiritual celebrity. We do the same thing in modern times with our celebrities. Most of our celebrities aren't religious leaders but movie stars and singers and the like. These are our modern gods; celebrity is what much of Western culture really worships. But just as a movie star eventually tires of the paparazzi and wants to get away, Jesus tires of the celebrity that comes from being a healer. He sees that it isn't serving his mission, so he begins to introduce a new teaching form—teaching in parables.

TEACHING IN PARABLES

9

> The seed of God is in us. Given an intelligent
> and hard-working farmer, it will thrive
> and grow up to God, whose seed it is; and
> accordingly its fruits will be God-nature.
>
> MEISTER ECKHART

Another form of teaching that Jesus utilized was the parable. The word *parable* comes from a Greek word meaning "comparison or analogy" and is essentially a very brief story that conveys a spiritual truth. A parable is a bit like a riddle: it has a meaning you can't completely understand with the logical, conditioned mind. A parable is meant to present your mind with something that pushes you to go beyond your current level of understanding in order to comprehend it. Different parables point out different states of understanding; some of them are fairly clear and understandable, while other ones are much more abstract.

TRANSMISSION AND DISCIPLESHIP

Parables were a common form of teaching in the ancient world and are especially important in the Christian tradition. There are many parables in the Gospels, but I want to focus on two in particular because I think they exemplify the whole tradition of parable stories and how they work. The first is the parable of the mustard seed. It's very short, so let's look at the entire parable, and then explore what it means.

> Again he said, "What shall we say the kingdom of God is like, or what parable shall we use to describe it? It is like a mustard seed, which is the smallest of all seeds on earth. Yet when planted, it grows and becomes the largest of all garden plants, with such big branches that the birds of the air can perch in its shade."
> With many similar parables Jesus spoke the word to them, as much as they could understand. He did not say anything to them without using a parable. But when he was alone with his own disciples he explained everything.
> [Mark 4:30–34, NIV]

This passage evokes the ancient tradition of insiders and outsiders. Jesus explained these parables to his disciples because they were the insiders, the ones he had chosen to understand his message. It was to these twelve insiders that he hoped to transmit—as we say in Zen—the truth of these stories. In many esoteric forms of spirituality, transmission from teacher to student plays a key role. The relative or surface way of understanding transmission is made clear in this parable. To transmit is to explain, to reveal the meaning of something. In a more esoteric sense, transmission is literally a type of resonance or awakened field of consciousness present within a spiritual master that can help activate spiritual awakening within another.

Because Jesus is enlightened, because he is established in the Kingdom of Heaven, his consciousness carries the resonant field of the Kingdom and can awaken it in those around him if they are open to him in a deep way. In esoteric spirituality—meaning those inner forms of spirituality concerned with awakening, transformation, and enlightenment—transmission plays a significant role. It's not something constrained by words or explanations, and it's not quite an energetic transmission either; it's a field of consciousness. Ultimately, Jesus' mere presence is his greatest teaching tool.

To make this a little clearer, imagine you walk in a room and there's one person in the room, just sitting in a chair and staring at the wall, deeply depressed. Now, just imagine if you were to walk through the door and then stop and just *feel* the presence of that room. If you were sensitive, you would literally feel the dark, heavy energy of the person in that room; you would feel their depression. That too is a kind of transmission, so transmission isn't necessarily as obscure as it might sound. It's really our capacity to feel, in some regard, what another is feeling. It is to partake of their state of consciousness. When someone is happy, their consciousness is bright, vital, and alive, and you can feel that brightness and vitality because their consciousness is literally activating the brightness and joyful aspect of your own consciousness.

Between a spiritual teacher and his or her student, transmission is the teacher's state of consciousness interacting with the consciousness of the student or the disciple. So in this story, Jesus is utilizing both forms of transmission. There's the ordinary or relative transmission, which is to explain or reveal the hidden meaning of a parable in a conceptual or intellectual way. There's also the more fundamental transmission of utilizing the power of his presence to awaken and transform others. This vitality center, this presence that Jesus uses to transmit wisdom is the same presence he used to heal people physically and spiritually.

Jesus is always using his presence, and he's using it in a particular way with his disciples. As I've said, his disciples are the ones he has chosen to work with closely. In the ancient world, philosophy and religion were not separated. In the modern era, philosophy has broken away and become an intellectual discipline of its own, but in Jesus' time philosophy and religion were essentially one and the same. As a student, you'd come to the teacher of philosophy or to the priest for your training, and they would choose when to reveal the hidden meaning of the teachings to you when they saw that you were ready to take the next step beyond the outer forms. When you were ready to peer behind the veil and see a deeper aspect of the teaching, then the teacher would pull you aside and make you one of the insiders.

This was done in ancient times and it's done today as well. The purpose isn't necessarily to create a division between insiders and outsiders. It's simply that there are certain spiritual teachings that can evoke states of consciousness that you don't necessarily want to subject someone to too early, because they may become too disoriented and frightened. The same awakening that for one person is liberating and uniting can be very frightening and disorienting for another person who isn't ready for it. In some extreme cases, the vibrational frequency of a higher state of consciousness can actually fracture the psyche and people can have a psychotic break. Usually it's temporary, but you never know for sure. So there are good reasons why someone like Jesus would be selective in the people that he brought close to him to reveal the deeper nature of his teaching.

PARABLES AND KOANS

Let's look at how Jesus actually describes his teaching in parables to his disciples. "The secret of the Kingdom of God has been given to you. But to those on the outside everything is said in parables so that, 'they may be ever seeing but never perceiving, and ever hearing but never understanding.'" [Mark 4:11–12, NIV]

There's a saying from the Sermon on the Mount in which Jesus warns not to cast pearls before swine. That's really what he's talking about here; he doesn't want to give the deepest teaching to those who are undeserving, either because they won't recognize it and will throw it away or because they aren't ready for it, and the mere magnitude of a spiritual opening might be more than they can take. In other words, for some it's best to continue with an outward form of spirituality until their emotional health and spiritual integrity becomes firmly established. Obviously, Jesus specifically chose the twelve disciples as people to whom he would transmit a much deeper teaching, and he chose to express his teaching in parables so that people couldn't understand exactly what he was saying unless they were in a deep state of readiness.

Zen Buddhism, the tradition in which I was trained, is very well known for utilizing the koan as a teaching tool. The koan is a kind of question or riddle, constructed in such a way that you cannot give the proper answer from your conditioned mind. In order to answer a koan correctly, you literally have to *become* and embody the koan. Perhaps the most widely known koan in our culture is: What's the sound of one hand clapping? We all know the sound of two hands clapping, but what's the sound of one hand? This is an example of a koan or riddle that you might be asked to meditate upon until the question, what is the sound of one hand clapping? becomes part of your consciousness. If you were to go back to your teacher and give them an intellectual answer, even if the intellectual answer was philosophically profound or coherent, in Zen it would easily be dismissed as the wrong answer. You'd be told to continue to meditate on the question until you have the actual experience of the sound of one hand clapping and you can then demonstrate that to your teacher.

As soon as we drop out of the conceptual mind, that part of the mind that's always abstracting our experience so that we're constantly living in our thoughts, we can become the question. Then the question penetrates to the very roots of our consciousness, and at some point we'll see that the entire universe is one hand clapping—that's what it actually *is*. Now, I can't explain that in intellectual terms, but that's the kind of understanding a koan points to. In Zen, you're meant to contemplate the koan, and you're not supposed to tell other people the answers that you've come to, so there's a secret tradition in Zen as well; the answers or the resolutions to koans are not to be published in books or given out to anyone else. Reading the answer to a riddle may give you an intellectual comprehension of it, but you still haven't actually become the answer yourself, and the whole function of a koan is to *become* the resolution of the question.

In a certain way, parables function similarly to koans. To understand a parable, you have to fully inhabit its meaning. And when you fully inhabit the meaning, then you've entered the Kingdom of Heaven, you've entered eternal life—your true nature, your deathless nature. In fact, the Gospel of Thomas begins with Jesus saying that those who understand his teachings will enter the Kingdom of Heaven and not experience death. These parables and teachings of Jesus can only be understood from the perspective of divine *being*, from the perspective of the Kingdom of Heaven—thus you must be in that state in order to understand them. There's a long tradition of constructing a teaching that can only be understood from the enlightened state. When one is in that state, all of a sudden everything makes sense.

THE PARABLE OF THE SOWER

So Jesus has gathered his disciples, the insiders to whom he's going to transmit the teaching. This is his hope, but it doesn't quite work out as he imagined. In this next passage, Jesus has just spoken to a large crowd gathered at the shore and shared with them the parable of the sower, which concerns the sowing of seed on different kinds of ground. Now he's alone with his disciples, and he finds that he has to explain the parable to them.

> Then Jesus said to them, "Don't you understand this parable? How then will you understand any parable? The farmer sows the word. Some people are like seed along the path, where the word is sown. As soon as they hear it, Satan comes and takes away the word that was sown in them. Others, like seed sown on rocky places, hear the word and at once receive it with joy. But since they have no root, they last only a short time. When trouble or persecution comes because of the word, they quickly fall away. Still others, like seed sown among thorns, hear the word; but the worries of this life, the deceitfulness of wealth and the desires for other things come in and choke the word, making it unfruitful. Others, like seed sown on good soil, hear the word, accept it, and produce a crop—some thirty, some sixty, some a hundred times what was sown.
> [Mark 4:13–20, NIV]

Now, in one sense this is an obvious teaching. If you give the gift of spirit, it's akin to casting seeds; if the seed lands on rocky ground, there's nothing for it to take root in. You might be happy to receive the teaching, or the transmission of reality, from heart to heart, but if you are rocky ground, you can't

117

sustain it. As soon as tribulation comes, as soon as difficulty comes, you will lose whatever has been given because it's not deeply rooted and embodied in your *being*. Next is the image of the seed being sown on thorny ground. This refers to those who can hear the teaching, but are so attached to themselves—to their egos, desires, fears, and outer things of the world—that their lust for outer things chokes out spirit. When you believe that ultimate satisfaction can be found by acquiring more riches or success in the world, then even if you're given the truth, even if you have a realization of divine *being*, sooner or later you will forsake it for something that you value more than the gift that was given. Finally, if the seed is thrown on good soil, then it grows and multiplies. When the seed of truth is transmitted to you and you receive it inside, if you're really ready for it, if it is your highest value, if it is what you want the most, it will bloom in you. The teaching, the transmission of unity will bloom in you thirty-fold, sixty-fold, a hundred-fold.

As a teacher, I've seen this to be true. That's why the very first point of my teaching is to help people clarify their aspiration. In other words, what do you want? What do you value? Because if you're not clear on what you ultimately value and where your allegiance lies, then even if you open up to the divine presence, your divided mind will instinctually turn away from it. You will throw it away almost without knowing you're throwing it away. There's a type of inner unification that occurs, where what you want and what you hold as most valuable is like an arrow pointed in one direction; it doesn't waver all over the place.

In the egoic dimension of consciousness we often have many competing wants. We want and value lots of things, and some wants and values are at odds with other wants and other values. An important part of spirituality is coming to a sense of clarity about what we ultimately want, what we ultimately value—and what we're willing to give up for it. And this is what Jesus is talking about in this explanation of this parable.

Jesus says that those who are rocky ground receive the word with joy, but because they have no root in themselves, when tribulation or persecution arises, immediately they fall away. It's interesting that, in Jesus' own life, when tribulation and persecution begin to occur, his own disciples prove themselves to be rocky ground. They all fall away, they all deny him, they all leave him when he is arrested, and this begins his inextricable movement toward the crucifixion. Yet each of those disciples experiences great joy when they first hear about the word, when they first hear and experience Jesus. Each one immediately responds and follows him. They seem to be the most ready, the most enthusiastic, the most unified in what they want. But when persecution and tribulation arise—which is exactly what Jesus ultimately goes through—they fall away. The seed dies on rocky ground.

Essentially, Jesus is telling his disciples: How is it that you don't understand what I'm telling you? As he says at the beginning of this passage, "Don't you understand this parable? How then will you understand any parable?" He's told them a very simple parable, yet his own insiders don't understand. Even when he tells them the deeper meaning, they *still* don't understand. So you can just imagine yourself in Jesus' place. You've gathered these disciples, these insiders, and you're going to transmit the teaching to them. Yet right from the beginning you realize, "Wow, they're rocky ground. They don't have the capacity to understand what I'm trying to teach them. As soon as I show them something, it just dies in them. They're enthusiastic at first, but as soon as there's any pressure, they revert back to their old mode of *being.*" It must have been very eye opening for Jesus when he realized that his chosen disciples couldn't make sense of such an easy parable.

TWO ORDERS OF *BEING*

This whole method of teaching in parables is not simply about insiders and outsiders, but more fundamentally it's about two different orders of *being*. Jesus' own disciples—as well as most of the people who come to see him—are functioning within the egoic realm of consciousness. Each thinks he is a separate somebody quite apart from the world around him, as well as separate from God. That's the state of consciousness they're in, and that's the state of consciousness that most human beings are in to this day. That viewpoint represents a certain order of *being*. Jesus, however, represents an entirely different order of *being*. He represents the Kingdom of Heaven, the enlightened state of *being*. This is why Jesus' own disciples cannot understand him; this is why almost *nobody* understands him. They're all walking around on the same soil, but what they perceive is *totally* different. They're of different orders of *being*, as different from each other as a caterpillar and a butterfly.

A caterpillar has the possibility of transforming itself into a butterfly, but until that transformation occurs, caterpillars are ground dwellers. They can climb up into a tree, but fundamentally they are limited to the horizontal domain. A butterfly can fly in the air; its sense of reality is *completely* different. A caterpillar can imagine what it's like to fly, but it can't experience flight until it undergoes that transformation. In a sense, Jesus is a butterfly. He's of a totally different order of *being*. Everyone he encounters is a *potential* butterfly, but to change, they first have to let go of everything they know, their entire sense of who they are, and their entire sense of who God is. Unless they do this, they cannot come up to the order of *being* that Jesus represents. To make this transformation, they must be clear; they must know what they want and be willing to step into a completely unknown dimension of consciousness.

And they must also be clear about what they're willing to relinquish. This is the line of demarcation. Many people say, "I'd love to be awake, I'd love to be enlightened." That's all well and good, but are you really ready to leave your old world behind? Are you really ready to leave your old self behind, or do you hope to bring the freedom of enlightenment down into your ordinary egoic dimension of *being?* In other words, do you want enlightenment as something that you can possess while you carry on with your life as you always have, or are you really ready to relinquish the life that you've known thus far? Nobody ever knows what's going to happen when they relinquish the life they've known, when they step into the mystery, into the transcendent presence that's peering through all the forms of time.

This radiance of consciousness is constantly peering through, presenting itself through all forms. And yet, when we're stuck in the world of form, in identification with body and mind, we're limited to a particular order of *being.* Even a deep spiritual revelation doesn't guarantee that we're going to live in that state that's been revealed to us. We have to be ready and willing when it comes. We have to want it enough that we're willing to give up whatever it takes to live in that new dimension of consciousness. One can never know how it's going to work out. It's always a leap of faith. Are you willing to take that leap of faith? Nobody can know what one's life will be like until they've made that leap. There are no guarantees of what will happen.

Throughout the Jesus story, we see his disciples struggling to take this leap of faith. They really want to experience the Kingdom of Heaven that he's talking about, and in their own way they're sincere, but whether they're ready or not is a completely different question. They seem to misunderstand him at almost every critical moment. These misunderstandings between Jesus and his disciples are a recurring theme throughout the gospel story, especially in Mark's gospel. And near the end of his life, his disciples will desert him because they're afraid of being persecuted. When push comes to shove, they all find out what they really value. They thought they valued what Jesus was trying to teach them, but in the end they were ruled by fear and doubt. And given the circumstances, you really can't blame them.

Again, this is a metaphor for one's inner *being*, for what we find when we look within. Things are not always as black and white as myth and metaphor present them to be. Most people have divisions about what they want and don't want. Most human beings are a combination of rocky ground, thorny ground, and good soil; we contain all these types of readiness within our hearts and minds. What's our allegiance to? What do we really value? Remember, what we value most is shown not by what we *say* we value, but by our actions—and that's made clear in this story. The disciples will say that they would go with Jesus anywhere. They believe they would never forsake him—but in the end they all abandon him. Their actions ultimately show what's in their hearts. I think this story holds up a mirror to the human heart and asks: What do you really see? Do you see a unified intention, or do you see split allegiances?

MIRACLES AND TRANSFIGURATION 10

> I am the light of the world. Whoever follows me will
> not walk in darkness, but will have the light of life.
>
> JOHN 8:12

Anyone familiar with the Jesus story can't help but to be fascinated by Jesus the miracle worker. To me, whether the miracles described in the Gospels really happened or not isn't ultimately an important question. A miracle is simply something we can't explain with rational thought processes or scientific analysis. From that perspective, miracles are very real. Even awakening itself, when it occurs, seems like a miracle. When we see with the eyes of divine presence, there are miracles everywhere.

MIRACLES ALL AROUND US

The more conscious we become, the more powerful we become. We don't necessarily become miracle workers, but as we begin to awaken and our state of consciousness opens, different capabilities within us come online and are available to us. As you come into harmony in life, then mysteriously, almost miraculously, life seems to come into harmony with you. There is a sense that everything is unfolding just as it needs to, that everything is right on time. As we let go of trying to control life, trying to force it in the direction that the ego wants it to go, life has a way of literally responding to our state of consciousness. And that's a miracle—that as your state of consciousness transforms, life's relationship with you transforms as well.

For some people that may seem like an outlandish idea, but it's just part and parcel of becoming more conscious. We cannot actually separate ourselves from life. All lines of separation are illusory. You can't remove a human body from its environment. Without the oxygen you breathe, you'll die. Without the warmth of the sun, you can't survive. The more conscious we become of the interconnectedness of all of life, the more life itself starts to work with us in a harmonious way. That's a miracle. How a human being can produce a baby, bring a beautiful little being into life—that's a miracle. When we focus only on big, extravagant miracles, we become unconscious to the fact that life itself is a miracle. The mere fact that there's *anything* rather than nothing is an absolute miracle.

Miracles are all around us; we just have to open our eyes and see. The more we open to the reality of our own divinity, the more we start to perceive life as a miraculous event. And though the miracles of our everyday lives may pass unnoticed by the self-obsessed mind, they are there nonetheless. It seems to me that a very intimate aspect of awakening is becoming aware of the daily miracle we move through, the miracle called life. Then, the big miracles of the kind we find Jesus undertaking can draw our attention to the miracle of our own lives.

I see the miracles depicted in the New Testament as being representative of deeper underlying realities. In other words, the miracles are themselves metaphors or teaching tools to hone our awareness, so we begin to become conscious of things in life and in ourselves that we usually aren't conscious of. All of the miracles in the Jesus story have what I'd call an ulterior motive; the point of the miracle isn't the miracle, but the underlying teaching that the miracle conveys.

JESUS CALMS THE STORM

The first miracle I want to discuss takes place when Jesus is crossing the Sea of Galilee by boat. Here's how the story reads:

> A furious squall came up, and the waves broke over the
> boat, so that it was nearly swamped. Jesus was in the
> stern, sleeping on a cushion. The disciples woke him and
> said to him, "Teacher, don't you care if we drown?"
>
> He got up, rebuked the wind and said to the waves,
> "Quiet! Be still!" Then the wind died down and it was
> completely calm.
>
> He said to his disciples, "Why are you so afraid?
> Do you still have no faith?"
>
> They were terrified and asked each other,
> "Who is this? Even the wind and the waves obey him!"
> [Mark 4:37–41, NIV]

There's an obvious miracle here, when Jesus rebukes the wind and the waves. I love this rebuke, this "Quiet! Be still!" This is the most potent spiritual practice—just to be quiet, to be still. When someone of spiritual maturity, like Jesus, says, "Quiet! Be still!" then things will be quiet and still.

Picture them together, in a boat in the midst of a furious storm: the disciples fearing for their lives, worried that the boat might overturn, while Jesus is lying in the stern of the boat, asleep on a cushion. This image shows with great clarity the difference between these two orders of *being*. Jesus is grounded in divine *being*, in that place from which everything is always perfectly ok. That center does not know fear; it does not know anxiety. That's the place where Jesus dwells. The disciples, on the other hand, move from the place of the ego. They are afraid for their lives and their base instinct is simply to survive. They are as unstable as the wind when they are overtaken by fear.

Now, the fact that they're on water is also fascinating. Earlier, I mentioned that water is the medium of the ethical and moral dimension and, in spiritual stories, it's also the medium of purification. In modern psychological terms, water indicates the unconscious. If you dream of being in water, for example, that dream indicates that you're accessing a deep place in your unconscious. So here is Jesus with his disciples, floating in a boat on the water, which represents the ethical and moral domain that most religions occupy. In its wildness and turmoil, it also represents the unconscious. This is a wonderful mythic image. I think everyone has experienced inner states full of anxiety, of turmoil, of emotions and fears that threaten to overwhelm them. In those moments, you struggle for equilibrium, trying to hold on to something that can give you peace, but your own psychology is quite out of your control; you can't command it to calm down unless you're of a different order of *being*.

Jesus is completely at ease floating upon the waters of the deep unconscious, which are filled with all those forces within ourselves that we usually try to hide from and to deny. Why is Jesus at peace in this realm? Because he's awakened *being*, and because he's dealt with all this before. He faced these forces in the desert, when he faced Satan—his demon, his own unconscious shadow. Jesus has been through all of this. He's found the center, and he knows what's ultimately most important to him. He's not fractured in his psychology or in his intentions. He is completely and absolutely unified, established at the still point of eternity within his own *being*, and thus he knows the unconscious is no threat to him no matter how dark the shadows, no matter how threatening or malicious they seem to be. The disciples are still caught in the world that swirls around the still point of eternity. They're in the relative world, and they're powerless. Jesus, however, has found the peace beyond all understanding. He can say to those waves of the unconscious, "be still," and instantly they will be still. The disciples could scream, "be still!" and it would have no effect.

It's similar to what can occur when you sit in meditation. Anyone who's sat in stillness knows what it's like when you're trying to be calm and at peace, but the mind and emotions are in turmoil and there doesn't seem to be anything you can really do about it. You can't control it; all you know is that you want it to stop. So you hold on to whatever meditative techniques you have in the hopes that it will help. Anyone who's meditated has had this sort of experience at some point or another—probably many, many times. But someone who has real dominion over the shadowy realm of the unconscious is not afraid of it. They know it, they've dealt with it, and when they say, "be still," there's perfect stillness. It's not a technique; it comes from a deeper state of consciousness.

As this story shows, Jesus belongs to the dimension of divine *being*, while his disciples belong to the dimension of egoic consciousness. Thus, Jesus has a hard time understanding his disciples. To him it's all so simple—why don't you just have faith? In his dimension it's no big deal. But to the disciples it's a big deal, to the point that Jesus stilling the wind and waves is more frightening to them than the storm itself. In terror they asked each other, "Who *is* this? Who is this person that we're following?" What they're really asking is, "What have I gotten myself in to?"

I think many people who have deeply engaged in their spiritual journey have had moments where they wonder, "Wow, what did I get involved in? What have I done?" At the beginning of the journey, it feels like *you* are chasing God, and that's something you can comprehend. But at some point, if you chase God long enough and sincerely enough, everything switches, and it feels like God is chasing *you*. And once God is chasing you, you realize the reins of your life are really no longer in your ego's hands. Some other force is now commanding your spiritual journey, and your life has given way to a new, transforming force, the force of spirit and fire. And spirit and fire, as we've said, are not predictable—you cannot control them. Once they've been released within you, they have a life of their own that's unpredictable.

Again, this whole story can be seen as a metaphor for something common to all human beings. When we read this only as a story about Jesus and the disciples, then we hold ourselves at a distance from it. But when we open to its deeper meaning, we see ourselves reflected back. Then we must ask ourselves: do I align myself with the energy field Jesus represents—that quiet, still place in the midst of turmoil—or do I get caught up in the waves of the unconscious, with all their fears and anxieties?

THE TRANSFIGURATION

The story I want to look at next is not a miracle in the sense of what Jesus does, but rather in the sense of what happens to him.

This is the story of the transfiguration. I think that by any definition the transfiguration is a miracle story, and what occurs is of enormous consequence and has enormous power, as we'll see. First let's read the story in its entirety as it appears in Matthew, as I think it's quite beautifully written.

> After six days Jesus took with him Peter, James, and John the brother of James, and led them up a high mountain by themselves. There he was transfigured before them. His face shone like the sun, and his clothes became as white as the light. Just then there appeared before them Moses and Elijah, talking with Jesus.
>
> Peter said to Jesus, "Lord, it is good for us to be here. If you wish, I will put up three shelters—one for you, one for Moses and one for Elijah."
>
> While he was still speaking, a bright cloud covered them, and a voice from the cloud said, "This is my Son, whom I love; with him I am well pleased. Listen to him!"
>
> When the disciples heard this, they fell facedown to the ground, terrified. But Jesus came and touched them. "Get up," he said. "Don't be afraid." When they looked up, they saw no one but Jesus.
>
> As they were coming down the mountain, Jesus instructed them, "Don't tell anyone what you have seen, until the Son of Man has been raised from the dead."
> [Matthew 17:1–9, NIV]

What actually occurs up on this mountain when Jesus becomes transfigured? What happens to Jesus when "his face shone like the sun, and his clothes became as white as the light"? The transfiguration is a part of spiritual unfolding that arrives at a particular point in the journey of awakening. It comes well after the initial awakening, after you've gone through trials—often years of trials—and met those trials from the state of divine *being*. These experiences have helped you come to a totally unified state, a state of abiding peace, of abiding tranquility. At that point, you may think, "Well that's all there is to it. I've arrived at this beautiful place of freedom." But there's still something else to come—what the Gospels call the transfiguration, a new and unexpected influx of spiritual energy.

It's very hard to describe exactly what happens in transfiguration; it's as if you fully become the radiance of divine *being*. You have to go to a deeper level than was required either for your initial awakening or for the trials and tribulations that followed. In a sense, you become a fully spiritualized being. This doesn't mean you no longer have a human component; there's still a human being there, every bit as much as there is in the Jesus story. But there is a shift—for certain people it's radical, as this story depicts, for others it's subtler. For Jesus, the transfiguration orients him completely toward his destiny, toward the fate of his life.

Prior to the transfiguration, Jesus obviously had access to the divine radiance in a deep and profound way; he utilized it in his healings and pointed toward it in his parables. But it is during the transfiguration that he fully becomes the radiance. He has become fully spiritualized right down to his physicality; he fully embodies divine *being*. The voice of God confirms: "This is my Son, whom I love; with him I am well pleased."

It's interesting that both Moses and Elijah were also on that mountain at the moment of his transfiguration—not as physical beings but as visionary witnesses to his spiritual unfolding. I had a similar experience on the very day of one of my profoundest awakenings, in my early thirties. I just wanted to be by myself on that day, so I went for a walk up on top of a hill—St. Joseph's hill—above an old Catholic Seminary building that had long since closed down. I'm not usually a visionary kind of person, but as I stood on that hilltop, I had a vision of Jesus, Buddha, and Yogananda. These were my deepest influences. I'd studied Buddhism for fourteen years, Christ had a huge impact on my life, and my wife had been raised in the teachings of Yogananda, a great Hindu sage and enlightened *being*. These three faces just appeared in the sky as I gazed out over the canyon below. I knew they were visions, that my mind was creating them, but still they were significant. It was almost as if they were there to witness what was occurring, to confirm what was unfolding, as when God speaks to Jesus in the transfiguration story, confirming "I'm pleased with you, you got it right."

THE SOURCE OF ALL LIFE

As I mentioned earlier, there are parallels and differences between Jesus and Moses in terms of how they express and relate to divine *being*. When Moses goes up the mountain, he meets God in the burning bush. In the Judaism of that time, God is seen as other. Moses will always be a human being, God will always be God, and the most that Moses can hope for is to have a correct, harmonious relationship with God. For Jesus, however, something very different happens. When Jesus goes up the mountain and meets the radiance of God, there's no relationship with the radiance. Jesus *becomes* the radiance; he himself is transfigured. The teaching contained within this story is not about *relationship* with God, but about identity as the divine itself.

Now, I'm very well aware that in Christianity as it has come down through the centuries, the exterior emphasis is about cultivating a right relationship with God, just as Moses did. Of course, even within this tradition that emphasizes having the correct relationship with the deity—with the vital source or the essence, you might say—for two thousand years there has also been an inner, esoteric tradition. In the tradition of the mystics, spirituality goes deeper than just having a relationship with God.

Earlier I shared a beautiful quote from Meister Eckhart: "The Father gives birth to his Son without ceasing; and I say more: He gives me birth—me, his Son and the same Son." You can see in this passage that Meister Eckhart is experiencing the Christ within himself, and asserting that he is the Son and that he and the Christ and God are of the same essence, the same such-ness. So even in the Christian tradition, with its emphasis on correct relationship with God, certain mystics went far beyond the notion of relationship and realized that, ultimately, Jesus was conveying something much deeper. Jesus' message is not so much one of having the right relationship *to* God as it is discovering the right identity *as* God.

Jesus breathed new life into the old Jewish tradition, taking it somewhere that it had not fully gone before. Every spiritual tradition needs someone to come along now and then to re-inspire it, to literally breath new life into it; otherwise, the tendency is for religious traditions to become too insular and constrained by the agendas of the relative world. Jesus' morality is not about right relationship; Jesus' ethical center arises directly and sponta-neously from divine *being,* from the source itself. It's not coming through an institution, and it isn't concerned with serving the relative needs and wants of human beings. This is what the trans-figuration shows: that there is a radiance that shines through all existence, and this radiance is the vitality source of all life.

On two occasions, I have had the experience of being with people who were within weeks or even days of death. When they realized they were going to die, they actually did what the ancient perennial spiritual teachings suggest—to die before you die, so that you can truly live. In other words, to completely let go while you're alive. To completely let go is to literally relinquish the survival instinct; if you let go at the deepest level, it's very much a type of ego death. Though their bodies were ravaged by disease, both these people were radiant, filled with vitality, and more alive than they'd ever been. And in both of those cases, they spent their final days comforting the people around them, because they no longer needed to be comforted. They were at peace with death. They knew that death doesn't take away the immortal divine *being*.

THE LIGHT OF EVERYTHING

For Jesus, Moses and Elijah appear in an ephemeral form, as witnesses to his transfiguration. As usual—especially in the Gospel of Mark—the disciples get it wrong and suggest putting up shelters for Moses and Elijah. Now, why would you put up a tent for a vision? They're already frightened and misreading what's happening. Next, the clouds gather, and the voice of God comes from above and gives its confirmation to Jesus. Of course, this terrified the disciples even more. They didn't know what to do. "Who's this guy we're following that God speaks to? What's this whole transformation about? Why is this guy glowing white with radiance?"

As the gospel story unfolds, Jesus discloses more and more of what he really is, and the disciples have a real problem getting it. It's as if Jesus' whole life is a kind of Zen koan, a riddle, and he only gradually displays what he is. Of course, metaphorically the story is showing what *you* are as well. All these ancient metaphors embedded within the Jesus story existed well before the time of Jesus. As I've said, it doesn't matter how much of Jesus' life is historically accurate. This story is speaking about you and me, about all of us. It's speaking about a reality that lives within us, waiting to be discovered. It's your true *being*, your true self. Your true nature *is* the radiance, and in this story the radiance and the human come together, just as they do in you and in me. Jesus shows the radiance of divine *being* appearing as human being. During the transfiguration it's all radiance, but as the story unfolds we will see that Jesus has some profoundly human moments.

As the transfiguration ends, Jesus says, "Don't tell anyone what you have seen, until the Son of Man has been raised from the dead." By this time, Jesus fully understands the trajectory of his life. His life is a physical manifestation of the journey of spiritual awakening. He's not writing about it; he's not teaching about it; there's not a thread of abstraction in the story of his life. He is *living* it. The events of his life are metaphors for spiritual transformation itself. He's living out in the flesh and blood what each human being has the potential to experience in their spirit. That's the beauty and the power of the story.

If we believe that it only has to do with Jesus and not with us, if we believe that he's the one and only God-man, then we misread the entire story. For two thousand years, this story has in large part been misread. When the early church decided, in AD 325, to establish the articles of Christian faith in the Nicene Creed, Jesus became the only begotten son. Less than three hundred years after the death of Jesus, the church fathers separated Jesus' reality from you and me. They said, "Only Jesus is the God-man. Only Jesus is a combination of divinity and humanity; the most that we can do is to have the right relationship with him." At that moment, the church itself cut humanity off from entry into its own transcendent *being*. It's amazing that it didn't ultimately work, that through the saints and sages and mystics of the church, that the radiance kept bursting through. People continued to discover that what Jesus realized was something they could realize too—and that Jesus was urging exactly this, in spite of church dogma saying it wasn't possible and even more that it was taboo.

There is a passage from the Gospel of Thomas that speaks directly to the transfiguration event in this story.

> Jesus said: "I am the light above everything.
> I am everything. Everything came forth from
> me, and everything reached me." [Gospel of Thomas 77]

Now, *that's* as clearly as the enlightened state can be put into words. I am the light of everything, the light of divine *being*, the light of consciousness. I am what lights up the world, I am what sees the world, and that seeing, that consciousness is actually what gives rise to the world. In some spiritual traditions, just to be the divine, eternal witness of all of life is enough; it's the goal. But in the spirituality of Jesus, that's *not* the goal. He doesn't say only, "I am the light above everything," but "I *am* everything; everything came forth from me."

The divine and the material realms collapse into each other, become each other. It seems as if they're reunited, but they were always one to begin with. It's just that we misunderstand and perceive division where there is none. The light above everything is that eternal still point within you that you can begin to intuitively sense at any moment. It's the part of you that has been the same for your whole life, from your earliest memory to this moment. It's what remains unchanged—the consciousness of your whole life. Everything that that light has seen and experienced has changed, but the light itself is the same light as it ever was.

If you really look, you'll find that spark of intuition that something about you is unchanging in the midst of all the change. That is the light above everything. That light has not been harmed; it has not been destroyed. Birth is not the beginning of that light, and death is not the end of that light. When that light fully comprehends its own nature, then it sees that everything came forth from that light and that it is everything. Everything—your hands, your face, the floor underfoot, the sky above, the birds, the flowers, the buildings, the cars, the pollution, the clear mountain lake—*everything* came forth from that light and is a manifestation of that light.

In the world of manifestation, sometimes the manifestation is a clear and transparent indicator of its source. Other times, manifestation gets confused in the human mind and comes out in destructive ways. But ultimately everything comes forth from that light and everything is that light. I call it the eternal formless form—that which in and of itself is nothing, but appears as everything. So anyone who has experienced this will see in this quote from the Gospel of Thomas a confession of their truest nature. Jesus is putting into words what the "I am" in all of us actually is.

In an awakened being, the divine presence is concentrated and luminous; it shines. It is no longer lost and obscured by the veil of unconsciousness. Such a one is no longer primarily a person but a presence. The personhood has been rendered transparent to the light of truth, the shining of divine being.

THE TRAJECTORY OF YOUR LIFE

For Jesus, the transfiguration was a profound experience that reoriented him toward his destiny. But each of us has a destiny. Each of our lives follows a certain trajectory, and there are moments when we see this deeply, even if for us it's not as dramatic as Jesus' transfiguration. And often the trajectory of our life is not what we expected. So much of life comes as a surprise; so much of what occurs in our lives is not what we intended. Life never unfolds like we imagine it will.

At certain moments, we have the ability to stand back and look at the overall arc of our lives. We ask ourselves: "What is my life really about? What am I serving?" You realize that you didn't consciously create your own life or connect all the dots, though in hindsight you may see great wisdom in the way it has unfolded. In those moments, you get a sense of the underlying direction of your life, whether it has to do with a particular role you are playing or a function that serves the greater good.

This is what I think happened for Jesus, though it isn't explicitly addressed in the text. Following the transfiguration, it seems clear that all of Jesus' actions consciously serve the unfolding of his destiny. He is going to be crucified on the cross; he is going to experience all the pain and suffering that leads to the crucifixion; he is going to go through the ascension. He knows all of this, and finally all of him can unite behind it and say, "Yes, this is my destiny, and I am going to live it out consciously and willingly."

SPEAKING TRUTH TO POWER

Jesus was, as I've said, a revitalizing force within the religion that he grew up in. At this point in the story, he knows his fate. He has no reason to hold back when confronting the religious institutions that have failed in their true task of connecting people to the truth of their *being*. Jesus was never afraid to speak truth to power, and shortly after the transfiguration, there's a passage that illustrates this—the scene in which he confronts the money-changers at the temple. It reads:

> And they came to Jerusalem. And he entered the temple
> and began to drive out those who sold and those who
> bought in the temple, and he overturned the tables
> of the money-changers and the seats of those who

sold pigeons. And he would not allow anyone to carry anything through the temple. And he was teaching them and saying to them, "Is it not written, 'My house shall be called a house of prayer for all the nations'? But you have made it a den of robbers." And the chief priests and the scribes heard it and were seeking a way to destroy him, for they feared him, because all the crowd was astonished at his teaching. [Mark 11:15–18, ESV]

This passage speaks to the necessity of the revitalizing force, not only in religion as a whole, but also within one's own life. Religion as a whole needs the renewing influx of true spiritual vitality from time to time. Enlightenment, real enlightenment, isn't containable; it doesn't fit nicely and simply into old, constraining structures. It's not that the revitalizing energy of spirit inherently rebels against all structures or against all authority. There are forms and structures in life that are very necessary, and there are institutions that can actually help people connect to the deeper nature of their *being*.

The forms and structures that religious and social institutions take on aren't problematic in and of themselves. However, they have a tendency toward inertia, a tendency to simply try to sustain the institution and positions of power of those within it. When any institution starts to become preoccupied with maintaining inertia so that the people within it maintain their positions and powers, then it starts to degrade. The life force begins to ebb out of the form. That's why, on occasion, it's important for someone to come along who can reinvigorate the religious institutions and bring the life force of spirit back into the old traditions.

That's the part Jesus is really playing here. If he simply wanted to have nothing to do with institutions, he would just walk away and not focus on revitalization. But clearly he is inspired to breathe new life into the religion that he grew up in. This image of Jesus entering the temple and overturning the money-changers' tables, strikes me as a vivid example of someone utilizing what you could call *holy rage*. He's had it. He's had enough of seeing the inner spirit of his religion be degraded by the institution. He's upset that the institution is being used for money and commerce, and has become more about merchandizing and maintaining power than about a transmission of the Holy Spirit.

When Jesus refers to the temple as a den of robbers, it's a profound critique. He's directly criticizing the Pharisees and the priests, which of course gets him into trouble. The Pharisees are the very ones trying to maintain their power, and they see that someone like Jesus is not containable or controllable. And so, they seek a way to destroy him.

This theme of those in power trying to destroy that which brings new life is a very common theme in Jesus' time, as it is in our own. Any group or institution has a tendency after a while to work more to sustain itself and the people who are in positions of power than to serve its original purpose and inspiration. This is not true only in religious institutions. We can see this in politics as well, when politicians no longer operate as noble servants of the people and instead start to serve their own ends, working to extend their own careers or rise to a higher place of power. They begin to turn away from their original calling, which is to serve the whole, to be the representative of a much larger group of people. We see this same dynamic of inertia and the corruption of power in many of life's institutions.

When institutions degrade in this way, it doesn't mean that there's something inherently wrong with them. They don't need to be destroyed; they need to be renewed and revitalized. And that spirit of renewal and revitalization is a real key to understanding the life of Jesus. He speaks truth to power, and by speaking truth to power, he opens up the way for a new energy to enter the institution—the energy of spirit, the energy of truth. This is one of the main functions in his life.

Shortly after the scene at the temple, Jesus offers another critique of religious authority.

> And in his teaching he said, "Beware of the scribes, who
> like to walk around in long robes and like greetings
> in the marketplaces and have the best seats in the
> synagogues and the places of honor at feasts, who
> devour widows' houses and for a pretense make long
> prayers. They will receive the greater condemnation."
> [Mark 12:38–40, ESV]

In this passage, Jesus is offering a critique of the spiritualized ego—the ego that's taken on a spiritual role and seeks fame, notoriety, and a higher status in society. Anyone who's been involved in any formal religion knows that you don't have to look far to find such people, who are forming a new self-image around their spirituality. The spiritualized ego gives us a nice, positive reflection of ourselves, and I think that a lot of us at some point in our lives have engaged in this. Many of us get involved in spirituality and find our path, and then, without our being aware of it, the ego starts to slowly co-opt that path. We begin to place more attention on appearing to be spiritual and talking about spiritual things than we do on the real heart of spirituality, which is about our connection to the transcendent mystery of existence—our own existence and existence as such. We should never forget that this is what spirituality is essentially about; everything else is window dressing.

Jesus has a keen eye for window dressing. He can see when the ego is pretending to be spiritual, and he speaks truth to that illusion, to that power. When he's giving this criticism, when he's saying, "beware of people like *this*," he might be talking to us. "Am I acting this way? Has my ego co-opted my spiritual search? Have I become more interested in *appearing* to be spiritual or holy than in really seeking the heart of the transcendent mystery? Am I personally ready and willing to be truly transformed?"

This transforming power of spirit is connected to the element of fire. This is what John the Baptist saw in Jesus, and this is why he said, "he who is coming after me . . . will baptize you with the Holy Spirit and fire." [Matthew 3:11, ESV] Fire burns away the old structures, the façades, and all that is illusory. It is a purifying force, a force that cuts much deeper to the bone than most people imagine. And the transformation that awakening can bring is much deeper than a lot of people may be prepared for. But Jesus understands the depth of this transformation, and he is ready to live out his destiny.

THE LAST SUPPER
AND THE GARDEN

11

> You should know that God must act and pour
> Himself into you the moment He finds you ready.
>
> **MEISTER ECKHART**

The next pivotal scene in the Jesus story is the Last Supper. Jesus has gathered his disciples together in a room, and a dinner has been prepared for them. It's an intimate scene, and quite poignant, because when the disciples arrive, they don't know that it's going to be the *last* supper, the last time they will all be with Jesus, their spiritual master. But Jesus knows—and he knows exactly what he's doing. After the transfiguration, he's come fully into alignment with his fate, he knows that his life itself is his teaching, and its trajectory will lead him to the crucifixion.

The disciples are not fully aware of this fate. Jesus alluded to it on a few occasions, suggesting to his disciples that he's preparing the way for his death and resurrection, but he hasn't really told them the whole picture or filled in all the details. So imagine, the disciples have all come to the Last Supper thinking it's going to be a time of profound intimacy with their spiritual teacher, and in fact it does begin this way. There's a beautiful scene at the beginning of the dinner when Jesus gives a profound spiritual teaching. This is what he says:

> And as they were eating, he took bread, and after
> blessing it broke it and gave it to them, and said, "Take;
> this is my body." And he took a cup, and when he had
> given thanks he gave it to them, and they all drank of it.
> And he said to them, "This is my blood of the covenant,
> which is poured out for many. Truly, I say to you, I will
> not drink again of the fruit of the vine until that day
> when I drink it new in the kingdom of God."
> [Mark 14:22–25, ESV]

Here, he's already alluding to not being with his disciples for very long. In this intimate scene, Jesus turns their shared dinner into a ritual, one in which he himself becomes the sacrificial lamb. In the Jewish religion of his upbringing, there was a tradition of sacrificing a lamb as an offering to God, but here, Jesus is recasting the ancient ritual by offering himself up to God as the ritual sacrifice. When he takes the piece of bread and says, "this is my body" and gives it to each of them, it's a very intimate thing. *This is my body.* What is the metaphor here? What does this giving of bread symbolize? What does it really mean to give of my body?

Notice Jesus is not explaining this ritual. Ritual is, in large part, better left unexplained; when we explain too much, it takes away the ritual's mystery and vitality. Yet by saying "this is my body" and giving that piece of bread, mystically Jesus is giving of his entire self, revealing what we call the mystical body of Christ.

Now, the mystical body of Christ isn't the human body. For all of us, the human body is born and lives and dies. The mystical body is a universal body, what I call divine *being*. It is without form and is timeless. It is the essence of who Jesus is, and it's the essence of us all. This mystical body of oneness is the sacred essence that we all share in common. It's what we really are—the mystical body of Christ.

This can only be partially explained; beyond that we have to experience it for ourselves. But this passage gives a clue as to what the mystical body is like. It's the true nature of form, not just of the inner life but also of the physical body. The physical body is really made out of spirit, of consciousness, of suchness, as they say in Buddhism. We are all one in the mystical body of Christ, and this is what Jesus is trying to transmit. He's saying, "Look, this is me. Take my mystical body into you. Become me as I become you." This is what it means to give of the mystical body.

After the bread comes the wine, and this wine is a very powerful symbol for the movement of spirit, of life force, of vitality. Think of blood, how it moves through our veins and carries the vitality to every organ, every muscle, every nerve ending in our bodies. When Jesus offers the wine and says, "This is my blood," he's saying, "Drink of my spirit, drink of my essence. Drink the living source of vitality, which is eternal spirit. Take me into you."

That's what a ritual can do, even if your mind doesn't understand it. A ritual is not *meant* for you to understand, to have a nice idea of what the ritual is about. If you think too much, your intellectual understanding gets in the way. But if you imagine yourself there with Jesus at that supper, then you are one of the disciples. This is the challenge of the story. You can't read the Jesus story from the outside and truly understand it. You can't understand it from the vantage of a spectator. You have to take it in to you and put yourself right there at that table alongside those disciples. They're sitting with their spiritual master—who has drawn them by his charismatic presence, amazed them by his ability to heal, baffled them by his use of parables, and frightened them by performing miracles, from walking on water to the transfiguration. They sense something amazing, something astonishing about him, and yet they haven't completely entered in to his domain; they haven't become what he is. Even in this very rich moment of the Last Supper, they still don't know exactly what to make out of him. He's performing this very intimate act; he's feeding them. Imagine somebody putting food into your mouth, like a parent placing food in a baby's mouth. Adults don't feed each other, but here he is, the master, feeding them ritually in order to convey a deeper truth. He wants them to understand who he is—not simply as a human being, but in his essence. By understanding him, they may come to understand what they truly are.

This theme of understanding is one that runs throughout the Gospels and particularly the Gospel of Mark. Mark tells us over and over and over that, if you can really understand the story and interpret it correctly, you too will enter the Kingdom of Heaven. But to understand the story in this way, you can't remain a spectator. You can't remain outside of it, in your theology or your belief systems. All that has to be left behind, so you can enter into it, and you enter into it by putting yourself into the story, by becoming the disciples, by becoming Jesus, by becoming the Pharisees, by becoming Satan, by becoming the radiance. When you throw yourself into the story, you may find out in a deep way what it means to you.

For me, the Lord's Supper has always been one of the most touching and poignant moments of the entire story. It's an initiation ritual to mystically join all of the disciples and Jesus together in spirit, but it's more than that—it's also the way that

Jesus begins to say good-bye. This supper starts with enjoyment and ease, as the disciples talked to one another, and then changes and deepens as Jesus moves into the ritual of offering his body as the bread and his blood as the wine. You can imagine how close together this ritual must bring them all and the charged presence in the room. In this spiritualized atmosphere, Jesus is enacting his final good-byes, though his disciples don't yet know it.

So just at the moment that he brings them the closest, that he draws his disciples to him and tries to pour himself out into them, there is an abrupt change. In Mark, Jesus speaks of betrayal at the meal's beginning, but in John he waits until the very end before he says:

> After saying these things, Jesus was troubled in his
> spirit, and testified, "Truly, truly, I say to you, one of
> you will betray me." The disciples looked at one another,
> uncertain of whom he spoke. One of his disciples,
> whom Jesus loved, was reclining at table at Jesus' side, so
> Simon Peter motioned to him to ask Jesus of whom he
> was speaking." [John 13:21–24, ESV]

Now, the beloved disciple is thought to be John; in the Gospel of John, John refers to the beloved disciple a number of times, and it's clear that he really means himself. John was particularly intimate with Jesus, and throughout the Gospels he is the disciple who seems to have the deepest understanding of Jesus. Though John will be one of the disciples to abandon Jesus after his arrest, nevertheless he has this real affinity for Jesus, and Jesus has an affinity for him. In some paintings of the Last Supper, he's shown reclining against Jesus, resting his head against Jesus' shoulder.

You can imagine the chaos and confusion it must have unleashed in the room when Jesus spoke of this coming betrayal. You can imagine the feeling, the tone in the room immediately darkening. As soon as Jesus says these words about betrayal, Peter asks John to find out which one will betray him. John is leaning against him, and Jesus whispers the answer in John's ear.

> So that disciple, leaning back against Jesus, said to him, "Lord, who is it?" Jesus answered, "It is he to whom I will give this morsel of bread when I have dipped it." So when he had dipped the morsel, he gave it to Judas, the son of Simon Iscariot. Then after he had taken the morsel, Satan entered into him. Jesus said to him, "What you are going to do, do quickly." . . .
> So, after receiving the morsel of bread, he immediately went out. And it was night. [John 13: 25–27, 30, ESV]

Now the Lord's Supper has become a completely different scene than it was at the beginning. The mood has grown dark and foreboding. Jesus has given an answer only to John, saying, "It is he to whom I will give this morsel of bread." Again, what an intimate thing to do—to feed another. And as soon as Judas takes the bread that Jesus has dipped and offered to him, the text reads, "Satan entered into him." So in a certain sense Jesus is initiating Satan's entrance into Judas. This is an unexpected turn; it isn't the conclusion that one would imagine when this intimate scene first began. It brings up lots of interesting questions. Was Judas actually malicious to begin with? Did he have the spirit of Satan in him? Or did Satan enter into him, as the text says, when Jesus put the bread into his mouth? This also brings up the issue of fate: did Judas have any choice in the matter? Are we all on our own trajectories of fate in our lives, with less choice in things than we think we have?

If Judas had no idea what the bread contained, then his taking the bread was an innocent act; you can't blame him for that act. Jesus by this point knows what's happening. He knows Judas is going to betray him, and he's just walking through the scenes now; he's just playing his part until his death; he's already seen how he's going to die. In a sense, Jesus is going through the motions, and Judas is helping him to write the conclusion of his life.

In other words, we can see Judas from different points of view. One point of view is the one we've inherited from the Christian tradition—that Judas is an evil man who betrays the savior of mankind. There is some indication that Judas had character flaws from the very beginning: he was stingy and was the most ill mannered of all the disciples, so he didn't have a great disposition to begin with. But whether he was actually evil or not we don't really know, though he's portrayed that way. We could also see Judas as the victim of circumstance. It could be that, in a script written long before, he was destined to play the part of Jesus' betrayer. Who exactly is Judas? Is he guilty, or is he helping Jesus live out his destiny? We aren't told any of this. This is what a great story or a beautiful myth evokes in us—a rich ambiguity. It doesn't fill in all the blanks; it doesn't explain everything to us.

I think, however, that we can all see a little bit of Judas in ourselves. Everybody has had the experience of betraying another, or maybe of betraying ourselves. Everyone at times has had the experience of feeling like you're at the mercy of an unfolding drama. Is it all fated from the beginning? Is it all written in stone, or can we make it up as we go and change our direction? These are the kinds of questions that the Lord's Supper brings up. It doesn't resolve them; instead, it provides a mirror in which we can see ourselves more clearly and move beyond the type of dualistic thinking that cannot embrace paradox.

YOU WILL ALL FALL AWAY

From the Last Supper on, the scenes move very quickly toward the crucifixion. One of the key elements of this portion of the story is Peter's denial, which Jesus predicts at the end of the Last Supper. Now, Peter is one of those guys who is always pretending to be more than he his. He really wants to be accepted, to be part of the in-crowd, and so he's always overplaying his hand, and we'll see this in this next scene. In Mark, this occurs immediately following the sacrament of the bread and wine.

> And Jesus said to them, "You will all fall away, for it is
> written, 'I will strike the shepherd, and the sheep will be
> scattered.' But after I am raised up, I will go before you
> to Galilee." Peter said to him, "Even though they all fall
> away, I will not." And Jesus said to him, "Truly, I tell
> you, this very night, before the rooster crows twice, you
> will deny me three times." But he said emphatically, "If
> I must die with you, I will not deny you." And they all
> said the same. [Mark 14: 27–31, ESV]

As we see here, Peter is just being himself. When Jesus says, "You're all going to end up denying me, you're all going to fall away," Peter is the one who stands up and says, "I won't. I'll never leave you." Peter makes himself a target for Jesus, and Jesus of course takes dead aim at him, saying, "Truly, I tell you, before the rooster crows twice you will deny me three times." Jesus knows Peter's persona; he knows if anybody is going to deny him out of weakness, it will be Peter. Peter is always trying to be someone he's not. He has what we might call a false bravado.

Of course, not only Peter but all of the disciples will eventually deny Jesus. These men have just had the Last Supper with Jesus, they've undergone this intimate ritual with him, and then the whole scene has turned in a very dark way as Jesus places the bread in Judas's mouth and sends him away. And now, Jesus is telling the disciples that all of them will deny him. So there's a real change in the tone at this point in the story. We are rushing toward the ultimate arrest and death and crucifixion of Jesus, and the whole story speeds up. The scenes come very, very fast now.

THE GARDEN OF GETHSEMANE

The story cuts quickly to the next scene, in the garden of Gethsemane. The passage begins:

> Then Jesus went with them to a place called Gethsemane, and he said to his disciples, "Sit here, while I go over there and pray." And taking with him Peter and the two sons of Zebedee, he began to be sorrowful and troubled. Then he said to them, "My soul is very sorrowful, even to death; remain here, and watch with me." And going a little farther he fell on his face and prayed, saying, "My Father, if it be possible, let this cup pass from me; nevertheless, not as I will, but as you will." [Matthew 26:36–39, ESV]

I find this one of the most touching moments in the entire story. This is a moment when Jesus, the Son of God, is being really human. Of course, he is divine and human, as we all are. Here at this critical moment, he has a foretaste of the torture he's going to go through. He understands that crucifixion is one of the most gruesome, painful, agonizing ways there is to die. It was not unusual during Jesus' time for people to be crucified, so he was very familiar with it. In this moment, facing his fate is very, very hard for the human side of Jesus, which I think anybody could understand.

Here's Jesus, the Son of God, begging God, "My Father, if it be possible, let this cup pass from me." Essentially, he's asking, "God, can I get out of this? Even though I know it's my destiny, even though I know I'm fated to do this, can I please get out of it?" That's a very human feeling, a very human emotion. And yet, immediately Jesus rights himself; he reconnects with divine *being* and says, "nevertheless, not as I will, but as you will." And right at that moment, he transitions from the purely human domain to the spiritual domain of divine *being* and spirit.

This scene, I think, says a lot about the totality of all of us. The human domain is fragile and fallible; the only certain thing about your life is your death. You never know what might happen—you could get seriously sick, or be in an accident, or a loved one could die—and these challenges can be extraordinarily difficult to get through. But Jesus shows a kind of courage even in the midst of this challenge. Right in front of his disciples, he falls to his face on the ground in sorrow. He's not trying to put on pretense or protect a persona or be a fake guru figure; he's a totally authentic being. When he's afraid, he's afraid, when he feels the urge to beg to get out of the situation, he does so.

But immediately, as soon as he says, "Yet not as I will, but as you will," he instantly returns and reconnects with divine *being*, with the will of God. This is a really important teaching. You can go off-balance—it's natural at times, given the intensity of certain experiences—but you can also reconnect with divine *being*, with the will of God, when you're ready and willing. So the story continues:

> And he came to the disciples and found them sleeping. And
> he said to Peter, "So, could you not watch with me one
> hour? Watch and pray that you may not enter into
> temptation. The spirit indeed is willing, but the flesh is
> weak." [Matthew 26:40–41, ESV]

Now, when I read these words, I believe he's not only talking to Peter, but to himself when he says, "The spirit indeed is willing, but the flesh is weak." This describes what he's experiencing right there in the garden. The flesh is weak—in other words, he wants to get out of his fate—but the spirit is willing. So, these words are not just a warning to Peter, but also a way that Jesus is confessing himself to Peter. He's saying, "Hey, I'm not as unlike you as you think I am. I have my human side. I have my frailty and my fears. Is it too much to ask for you to stay awake and be with me and watch over me? Did you really need to sleep so badly?"

There are moments in life that are charged with a spiritual vitality, when the veils between the time-bound world of ego and the timeless world of spirit become imperceptibly thin. These spiritually charged moments are critically important to recognize and respond to when they arise, as the Jesus story makes very clear. The Jesus story is an unending sequence of spiritually charged moments, occurring one after the other in quick succession from the beginning to the end. Jesus has a keen eye for such pivotal moments and knows instinctually how to respond when spirit moves, while his disciples either misread these moments or miss them all together. There is no better illustration of this than the disciples falling asleep in the garden of Gethsemane.

Again, for the second time, he went away and prayed,
"My Father, if this cannot pass unless I drink it, your will
be done." And again he came and found them sleeping,
for their eyes were heavy. So, leaving them again, he
went away and prayed for the third time, saying the
same words again. Then he came to the disciples and
said to them, "Sleep and take your rest later on. See, the
hour is at hand, and the Son of Man is betrayed into the

> hands of sinners. Rise, let us be going; see, my betrayer
> is at hand." [Matthew 26:42–46, ESV]

There's something going on in this charged atmosphere. We can see this scene as the real beginning of the Passion, Jesus' trajectory towards the cross and crucifixion. Here is the Son of God, the disciples' spiritual master, at a critical moment, in one of his most dramatic expressions of his human side. Three times he begs God to get him out of his fate, and three times he then accepts his fate, saying "Your will be done." This scene shows his human frailty, but also his capacity to realign himself through prayer.

There's something important in how the disciples keep going to sleep. Jesus isn't really asking too much when he asks his disciples to stay awake while he prays, but it's as if some force is pushing down upon them, making them go more and more and more unconscious. At the critical moment they can't stay awake, they can't stay fully conscious. This is the pivotal time, as Jesus' real fate begins to unfold, and this is when he *needs* the disciples more than ever. And yet, there seems to be a cosmic force that makes them literally go to sleep. They simply can't stay awake.

When we're in a very spiritually conscious, charged environment, there is part of the ego that tends to shy away and may literally go to sleep in order to avoid such a conscious environment. This is what the disciples are experiencing. They're going to sleep at the most profound and pivotal moment of their master's life and—though they don't realize it—the most profound and pivotal moment of their *own* lives, because they are just about to betray their spiritual master.

THE ARREST

No sooner has Jesus said the words, "my betrayer is at hand" than Judas appears, followed by a crowd sent by the priests. The authorities have given Judas money for betraying Jesus, and he has told them he will point out Jesus with a kiss.

So Judas comes up to Jesus and kisses him on the cheek as a sign to the authorities that this is the man they seek. Now, I find this a very curious way to point out someone that you are betraying. Usually one would want to keep their distance from someone that they are betraying; they would want to point them out from a distance. But Judas points out Jesus with the intimacy of a kiss.

This can be read in different ways. You could see the kiss as malicious, even evil, as if Judas enjoyed turning him in to the authorities and relished his role as the one who betrayed Jesus. But you could also see this as Judas following through on the path he was fated to follow when he received the bread from Jesus. This kiss on the cheek might be a way of conveying a real affection and tenderness for Jesus, as if to say, "Yes, we're both fated, we both have our destiny to play out, and I still love you."

As always in these powerful and mythic stories, they're trying to show us—you and me—something about ourselves. We've all experienced something of the betrayer in ourselves, that which would betray another for our advantage. We've all experienced that place in the egoic mind and heart that almost celebrates the misfortune of others. Many comedic movies have an element of this. And we've all, at times, felt as though we were playing out some sequence of events that felt in some way destined. The kiss may be acknowledging that sometimes fate dictates that we go through with our assigned roles. The kiss may even signal deep affection coming from Judas, as if to say, "You know, we're in this together, playing out our assigned roles."

I'm reminded of something my grandfather would do when I was a little kid. My grandfather was part Native American, and he had beautiful dark skin and jet black hair. Sometimes when we went to his house as kids, he would hop up off his chair, and he would start doing these Indian dances—or at least that's what we thought they were at the time. He would walk in circles around us chanting, "Hoya, hoya, hoya, hoya," and of course we thought it was quite hilarious. We loved watching grandpa do this strange dance because it was so funny to us.

Many years later, when I was in my thirties, an aunt of mine asked me, "Do you remember when grandpa would do those Indian dances in the living room when you kids came to visit?" And of course I remembered. My aunt said to me, "You know, he never told you this, but those were Indian dances of blessing." He didn't tell us because he didn't have to tell us; he just did it. We thought he was just being funny, but he was blessing us. You could interpret that gesture when Judas kisses Jesus' cheek as a blessing acknowledging that he is helping Jesus to live out his destiny.

In this kind of mythic story, you don't know the correct interpretation. You could see Judas as the personification of a kind of malicious evil, or you could see Judas as someone who was just doing what he was fated to do, as if he and Jesus were partners in Jesus' ultimate destiny, his death on the cross. From that perspective, then, you would see the kiss as something more affectionate. I think both possibilities are there in the story, and both interpretations can tell us much about the human condition.

PETER'S DENIAL

When Jesus is taken into custody by the authorities, his disciples desert him and flee from Gethsemane. Now that Jesus has been arrested, they know they're all in trouble. The authorities take Jesus to the high priest, and Peter follows at a distance, right into the high priest's courtyard, where the next scene takes place. Remember, Jesus has already foretold Peter's denial, saying,

"Before the rooster crows twice, you will disown me three times."
Here is how the Gospel of Mark recounts what happens next:

> And as Peter was below in the courtyard, one of the
> servant girls of the high priest came, and seeing Peter
> warming himself, she looked at him and said, "You also
> were with the Nazarene, Jesus." But he denied it, saying,
> "I neither know nor understand what you mean." And
> he went out into the gateway and the rooster crowed.
> And the servant girl saw him and began again to say to
> the bystanders, "This man is one of them." But again he
> denied it. And after a little while the bystanders again
> said to Peter, "Certainly you are one of them, for you are
> a Galilean." But he began to invoke a curse on himself
> and to swear, "I do not know this man of whom you
> speak." And immediately the rooster crowed a second
> time. And Peter remembered how Jesus had said to him,
> "Before the rooster crows twice, you will deny me three
> times." And he broke down and wept. [Mark 14:66–72, ESV]

This is a heartbreaking scene. At the beginning of Jesus' ministry,
Peter had enthusiastically dropped his old life to follow Jesus
and become one of his disciples. He assured Jesus that he would
never betray him, even unto death. Now, at this crucial moment,
he's in the courtyard warming himself by a fire, on the periphery
of Jesus' arrest and imprisonment, when a girl recognizes him
and says, "Hey! You are one of them!" And he says, "No, no,
no, I'm not one of them." By denying Jesus, Peter is in a certain
sense playing out his role, but he's also playing out his nature.
Remember, earlier in the story, in the parable of the sower, Jesus,
alluding to his disciples, said: "You are rocky soil. When the time
of tribulation comes, you will fall away, and you will deny me."

Of course, the disciples all had great hope when they rallied around Jesus. He was an amazingly charismatic spiritual figure, and you can imagine how exciting the adventure must have been when they left home and family to follow him. More and more people gathered around Jesus and amazing things happened: he performed miracles of walking on water, of calming the seas, of pulling demons out of people and casting them away. Jesus was a powerful miracle worker, and his spiritually enlightened presence inspired all his disciples.

And then, in a fairly short span of time, it all started to fall apart. You can imagine the shock, the disappointment, the absolute confusion the disciples must have felt as this powerful, charismatic being is arrested and dragged away to prison. What has become of your master? What has become of your life? What do you believe in now? What do you have faith in? Peter is a symbol; he stands for that within each of us that lacks faith, that lacks trust. He stands for that in us that pretends to be too strong, too boisterous—a bravado that is just covering over a human weakness and fallibility.

Peter's afraid that if he's associated with Jesus he might be arrested and dragged off to prison. This is one of those pivotal moments we find woven into scene after scene of the Gospels, where the deeper meaning can become very personal: What do *you* do at the pivotal moments of *your* life? When it really means the most, what are you going to decide is most important to you? It may be not what you imagined; you may overestimate or underestimate yourself.

For much of the story, what we see is how Jesus is moving through the world, the kind of decisions he makes, the way he rises up at those pivotal moments and orients himself toward the timeless expression of divine *being* and acts with great confidence and certainty. And now, in this transition, the same sort of certainty is being asked of the disciples. But they have not yet come into the order of *being* that Jesus lives from; when push comes to shove, they revert back to their familiar egoic identities.

Peter's denial is a representation of how we can turn away from our deeper nature of divine *being*. We may turn away out of pain, or sorrow, or betrayal, or some sort of abuse—anything in our experience that causes us to see ourselves as less than we truly are. There are many ways that human beings turn away from and deny their deeper nature. We turn away from the light and into the darkness, because sometimes the light is hard to bear. It's a myth that the light of *being* is always easy to bear; sometimes the radiance of the divine asks us to do difficult things. To remain oriented toward the spark of divinity within us is not always easy, and to act from that space can take great courage and faith.

This is what embodying one's spiritual realization is all about. We can have a great realization, but can we manifest it at the moments in our lives that matter most, both great and small? Do we embody the radiance of spirit, or is it simply a passing experience? The whole Jesus story is the story of embodied spirit, of what it means and what it looks like to embody and act from divine *being*. Peter stands for everyone who has ever turned away from the radiance, from truth, from their true *being*. Peter's not a bad man or malicious. In fact, he's extraordinarily well intentioned. But he hasn't yet found the Kingdom within himself, and so at the critical moments he's not capable of acting from the stillness of truth in a fearless way.

THE TRIAL OF JESUS

12

> Jesus said, "The foxes have their holes and
> the birds have their nests, but the Son of Man
> has no place to lay his head and rest."
>
> GOSPEL OF THOMAS

After the high priests question Jesus, they bring him to Pontius Pilate, the Roman governor of Judea. The trial of Jesus at the hands of Pilate is one of the most intense and rich scenes in the entire story. Pontius Pilate is going to ultimately decide the fate of Jesus, whether he wishes to or not.

KING OF THE JEWS

Outside Pilate's palace an angry crowd has assembled, made up of the priests of the temple and the teachers of the law. They are enraged with Jesus, for he has been nothing but a disruptive presence threatening their power and exposing their hypocrisy. From their perspective, he's offensive simply because he's his own man, his own authority. He's not driven to blindly follow the rules and regulations of the religion to which he was born. As a person of spirit, he values truth and freedom above all else. His God-given authority is threatening to the entire religious institution of the time. Seen mythically, this has nothing to do with Judaism. Jesus would resist the corrupt power dynamics of any religious institution. It just happens to be that he's a Jew, and so his criticism is directed at those in the Jewish hierarchy who are abusing their positions of power. When this scene begins, Pilate has gone outside to speak to the crowd that is calling for Jesus' death:

> So Pilate went outside to them and said, "What accusation do you bring against this man?" They answered him, "If this man were not doing evil, we would not have delivered him over to you." Pilate said to them, "Take him yourselves and judge him by your own law." The Jews said to him, "It is not lawful for us to put anyone to death." This was to fulfill the word that Jesus had spoken to show by what kind of death he was going to die.
>
> So Pilate entered his headquarters again and called Jesus and said to him, "Are you the King of the Jews?" Jesus answered, "Do you say this of your own accord, or did others say it to you about me?" Pilate answered, "Am I a Jew? Your own nation and the chief priests have delivered you over to me. What have you done?" Jesus answered, "My kingdom is not of this world. If my kingdom were of this world, my servants would have been fighting, that I might not be delivered over to the Jews. But my kingdom is not from the world." [John 18:29–36, ESV]

Pilate is trying to get to the heart of why these people are so upset with Jesus. First he asks the crowd, but they have no specific charges against Jesus. So Pilate asks Jesus, "What is it you have done?"

And Jesus simply answers, "My kingdom is not of this world." This is an odd answer to the question, "What have you done?" It almost doesn't even seem to fit. It's really pointing back to Pilate's earlier question, "Are you the King of the Jews?"

And Jesus' answer points to a theme we find throughout the story: "If my kingdom were of this world, my servants would have been fighting, that I might not be delivered over to the Jews. But my kingdom is not from the world." At the very beginning of the story Jesus descends from a timeless realm and comes into the world of time and space through the virgin birth. He's of a totally different order of *being*. He's not *of* the earth; he's not *of* the dualistic elements coming together; he's almost like a sacred principle—the divine principle incarnated in Man. His reality is that he came from another place, from which he brings the sacred spirit, the animating force of existence. That's his Kingdom of Heaven. That's what he embodies and brings forth. Jesus represents something far different than the world of duality would create—whether that's the world of politics or of the religion in which he was raised.

> Then Pilate said to him, "So you are a king?" Jesus
> answered, "You say that I am a king. For this purpose
> I was born and for this purpose I have come into the
> world—to bear witness to the truth. Everyone who is of
> the truth listens to my voice." [John 18:37, ESV]

In answering Pilate, Jesus is distilling down the essence of his mission. He is realizing exactly what his life is all about and has always been about. From the moment of the transfiguration he's been completely clear about his life's direction; he knows his fate, and he knows what he is here to accomplish. And he says it in this very simple but very powerful way, "The reason I was born and came into the world is to testify to the truth."

Here, Jesus is equating the Kingdom of Heaven with truth. And Pilate—being a man of the world, a man of politics, a man of great learning—is curious. Jesus' response is so unexpected that all of a sudden it sparks something in Pilate, and he asks, "What is truth?"

> Pilate said to him, "What is truth?"
> After he had said this, he went back outside to the Jews and told them, "I find no guilt in him. But you have a custom that I should release one man for you at the Passover. So do you want me to release to you the King of the Jews?" They cried out again, "Not this man, but Barabbas!" Now Barabbas was a robber. [John 18: 38–40, ESV]

The custom was that at each Passover the governor would pardon a prisoner; he would set free anyone the Jews want to be released. So Pilate here is trying to get out of this tricky situation he finds himself in. He has an angry mob wanting Jesus to be put to death, and as governor, Pilate is entrusted with maintaining the harmony of the state. That's his highest calling; it's what his life is about. So he's put in a difficult position by this group of citizens who are calling for the death of Jesus, when Pilate himself, in talking to Jesus, doesn't believe him guilty of anything. "I find no basis for a charge against him," he says. So Pilate goes to the crowd and offers to set Jesus free, but they reject his offer, and ask for the criminal Barabbas instead. The story continues:

Pilate went out again and said to them, "See, I am
bringing him out to you that you may know that I
find no guilt in him." So Jesus came out, wearing the
crown of thorns and the purple robe. Pilate said to
them, "Behold the man!" When the chief priests and
the officers saw him, they cried out, "Crucify him,
crucify him!" Pilate said to them, "Take him yourselves
and crucify him, for I find no guilt in him." The Jews
answered him, "We have a law, and according to that
law he ought to die because he has made himself the
Son of God." When Pilate heard this statement, he was
even more afraid. He entered his headquarters again and
said to Jesus, "Where are you from?" But Jesus gave him
no answer. So Pilate said to him, "You will not speak to
me? Do you not know that I have authority to release
you and authority to crucify you?" Jesus answered him,
"You would have no authority over me at all unless it had
been given you from above. Therefore, he who delivered
me over to you has the greater sin." [John 19:4–11, ESV]

This is a really fascinating moment. Once again, Pilate is trying to engage Jesus in conversation, and he's working hard to
come to a peaceful resolution to the situation. This is such a rich
exchange, where Pilate is trying to get Jesus to understand his
power to free or kill him, and Jesus answers, "You would have no
authority over me at all unless it had been given you from above."

This exchange reminds me of an old Buddhist story that contains a similar teaching. In ancient times there was a small village
with a monastery nearby. One day, samurai warriors arrived and
sacked the whole village. They took all the valuables, burned the
homes, and killed all the people they met. Finally, they came to
a monastery, and out in front of this monastery was an old Zen

master. He is just sitting in the garden when a young samurai warrior comes up to him. The samurai pulls out his sword, holds it up over his head and says, "Old man, don't you know that I have the power to kill you? I could lop off your head right now without even thinking of it."

And the old man just looks up at him and replies, "Don't you know that I could allow you to cut off my head right now without thinking of it?"

Now, at this the warrior drops his sword to his side for a moment. He's never met someone who had no fear of his own death, and so this old man intrigues him. And the old man says, "Oh, look at how weak you are." So once again the samurai lifts the sword over his head, and the old Zen master looks up at him and says, "That's hell." These words strike the samurai, and again he drops his sword; and the old man says, "And that's heaven." With that, the warrior bowed to the old Zen master and left him in peace.

Pilate here is like the samurai. He thinks that he's in the position of power. He's asking Jesus these questions, but Jesus isn't answering. Finally Pilate says, "Don't you realize I have power either to free you or to crucify you?" But Jesus is not operating from that human dimension. He's not afraid of whether he's killed or not, because he is living out his destiny, his calling. Jesus knows that this very moment is part of his destiny. As he's told Pilate, "You would have no power over me if it were not given to you from above." It's as if Jesus knows that this whole undertaking is a scripted moment, that it's just fate unfolding itself, and so he's completely aligned behind it. When someone is aligned with their fate in this way, it gives him or her a real sense of invulnerability, a sense of fearlessness and purpose. You sense that Pilate is both frightened and confused by Jesus, because he embodies a kind of fearlessness that Pilate has never met before in his life. Pilate has the power to take life, while Jesus has the much greater power to fearlessly give his life. The story continues:

> From then on Pilate sought to release him, but the Jews cried out, "If you release this man, you are not Caesar's friend. Everyone who makes himself a king opposes Caesar."
>
> Now it was the day of Preparation of the Passover. It was about the sixth hour. He said to the Jews, "Behold your King!" They cried out, "Away with him, away with him, crucify him!" Pilate said to them, "Shall I crucify your King?" The chief priests answered, "We have no king but Caesar." So he delivered him over to them to be crucified. [John 19: 12, 14–16, ESV]

You can see the chess match going on between Pilate, who wants to release Jesus, and the chief priests, who want him dead. Pilate sees Jesus as an innocent man—and perhaps he's beginning to believe that Jesus is truly the king of the Jews. These chief priests are very smart, very wily. They strike right at Pilate's weak point: as the Roman governor, he is entrusted with keeping the peace and ensuring that no one usurp his power—or the power of the emperor, Caesar. So when the Jews accuse Jesus, they say, "Hey, you have to kill him because he claims to be king of the Jews, and nobody can be king over Caesar." It's a strategic maneuver to push Pilate into a political corner so that he *has* to crucify Jesus.

So Pilate asks the crowd, "Shall I crucify your king?" And here the chief priests really reveal their bitterness and deceit. They show themselves to belong to a very low order of *being* when they say, "We have no king but Caesar." That's their way of saying, "We belong to the world. We will sell out our religion in order to make this crucifixion happen; we'll say that Caesar is our king."

There's something important to understand at this point in the story. Of course, this action is occurring between Jesus, Pontius Pilate, and the Jewish chief priests—but it's critical that we see the Jewish religious authorities mythically, not historically or factually. The Jewish leaders in this story stand for *any* religious authority that is corrupt, any religious authority that fails in its primary duty to connect people to the transcendent mystery that shines through all of life. So in this sense the chief priests stand for all forms of religion that have become corrupt. This is really important to understand because, in the past, the Gospel of John and its attitude toward the Jews have been used to justify anti-Semitism.

But when we look at the story mythically—as something that can show us the archetypes of the spiritual journey—then how the author of the Gospel of John felt about the Jews is unimportant. When we read the story mythically, we can even think of many Christian churches today as a modern counterpart to the Jewish religious authorities. I imagine that if Jesus walked into any number of the Christian churches today, he would be just as critical of them as he was of the Jewish temples and synagogues of his day.

Now the priests have forced Pilate's hand, and he feels he has no choice but to crucify Jesus:

> So he delivered him over to them to be crucified. So
> they took Jesus, and he went out, bearing his own
> cross, to the place called the Place of a Skull, which in
> Aramaic is called Golgotha. There they crucified him,
> and with him two others, one on either side, and Jesus
> between them.

Pilate also wrote an inscription and put it on the cross. It read, "Jesus of Nazareth, the King of the Jews." Many of the Jews read this inscription, for the place where Jesus was crucified was near the city, and it was written in Aramaic, in Latin, and in Greek. So the chief priests of the Jews said to Pilate, "Do not write, 'The King of the Jews,' but rather, 'This man said, I am King of the Jews.'"

Pilate answered, "What I have written I have written."
[John 19:16–22, ESV]

Pilate feels he has no other option but to put Jesus to death, but he leaves this one little clue about his feelings: the inscription on the cross, *King of the Jews*. Now, did he write those words on the cross to purposely upset the religious hierarchy, or did he write that because he had come to believe that Jesus indeed was the King of the Jews? The story can be read either way, or both ways. But by this point in the story, Jesus' fate is sealed. Pontius Pilate wants nothing more to do with the matter. His hand has been forced, and he's obviously upset about it. He says, "What I have written I have written," and that's the end of the conversation.

THE CRUCIFIXION

13

> Let nothing disturb you. Let nothing frighten
> you. Everything passes away except God.
>
> ST. THERESA OF AVILA

As we look at the crucifixion, I want to turn from the Gospel of John to the Gospel of Mark. Mark's telling of the story of Jesus' crucifixion is brief and intense. In fact, its brevity helps convey its intensity.

THE DEATH OF JESUS IN THE GOSPEL OF MARK

In the Gospel of Mark, Jesus' final moments are depicted like this:

> And when the sixth hour had come, there was darkness
> over the whole land until the ninth hour. And at the
> ninth hour Jesus cried with a loud voice, "Eloi, Eloi,

lema sabachthani?" which means, "My God, my God, why have you forsaken me?"

And some of the bystanders hearing it said, "Behold, he is calling Elijah." And someone ran and filled a sponge with sour wine, put it on a reed and gave it to him to drink, saying, "Wait, let us see whether Elijah will come to take him down."

And Jesus uttered a loud cry and breathed his last. And the curtain of the temple was torn in two, from top to bottom. And when the centurion, who stood facing him, saw that in this way he breathed his last, he said, "Truly this man was the Son of God!" [Mark 15:33–38, ESV]

In Mark, that ends the crucifixion scene. It's a very intense ending, with these twin cries of Jesus in the last moments on the cross, first "My God, my God, why have you forsaken me?" and then his wordless death cry. Now imagine if you can that you are Jesus, and you've led this very dynamic and God-filled life— the spirit descending upon you, undergoing trials in the desert, gathering the disciples, becoming a miracle worker and healer, speaking in strange parables—and now your life culminates in these words: "My God, my God, why have you forsaken me?" These are the last words Jesus will ever utter.

If we view the death of Jesus as it's depicted in the Gospel of Mark as part of the journey of spiritual awakening that we talked about earlier, we'll see that the crucifixion signifies a very profound point in one's spiritual evolution. The crucifixion is a symbol or a metaphor for a very advanced state of spiritual development, of spiritual consciousness. Now, when I first read how Jesus' death is depicted in Mark, it struck me very deeply. I felt like this depiction of the end of Jesus' life was really a representation or a metaphor for a very profound point in one's spiritual unfolding—and that is what I call "the death of self."

To understand what the death of self means, first we have to see how it's different from earlier stages of the spiritual journey. At the beginning of this process, when we first have a spiritual awakening, we transcend the ego. We go up and out of identification with the ego, the body, and the mind, and we realize our true nature as divine *being*.

Now, when you transcend something, it doesn't mean that what you transcended goes anywhere. And so we move into the time of the trials, when life gives us these situations that help us to practice and begin to embody what we've realized. Once we've gone through the many trials that teach us to embody spirit—and this stage often lasts for some years—we come to a deep and profound sense of resting, of ease, of well-being.

Then, following the gospel story, the next step is the transfiguration. Out of our deep peacefulness and serenity, we're suddenly struck by this new energy, this spiritual force. We *become* the radiance in a very profound way, and we embody the shining element, the openhearted element of spiritual realization in a way that we hadn't before. Of course, when this happens there's a new influx of life, a new influx of vitality. But at that same moment, there's a turning in which we clearly see our role in life. This moment comes for us individually, and it certainly came for Jesus: following the transfiguration, Jesus had a really clear sense of who he was, what his destiny was, and what role he was going to play in life. He had discovered, in full measure, his spiritual autonomy.

Jesus is one of the most alone figures in all of spiritual literature. As I've said many times, almost nobody understood him, and through all the critical moments of his story he was alone. Even when surrounded by his disciples, at those moments where he really needed their human support and human love, they couldn't stay awake for him. He went through his whole trial alone, his disciples disowned him, and it seems like the whole world was against him.

The transfiguration is really the discovery of a type of autonomy—not a sense of isolation, but a deep and profound sense that you're really standing in your own two shoes. One of my teacher's definitions of enlightenment was simply "standing in your own two shoes." It sounds easy, to stand up in our own life, but in order to really do it, first the divine radiance has to burn all the old conditioning that opposes spirit out of our system. This conditioning goes very, very deep; it alters all of our perceptions, all of our thoughts, our entire orientation to life.

To have that conditioning not merely transcended but literally burned out of our system—that's really what the transfiguration is all about. This is the death of the ego. And when that happens, something extraordinarily unique can begin to bloom in you. What blooms in you is not a product of the past; it's not a product of simply what you've experienced up to that moment; it's not a product of your culture, of your society, of your religion. It's the way that spirit manifests when it's no longer being confined by any conditioned view. This is what the transfiguration symbolizes.

Now when we come to the crucifixion, we're coming not just to the transcendence of ego or even the death of ego, which often takes place during the transfiguration. Now we're talking about the death of self. The clue that the end of Jesus' life signifies the death of self is found in the words he speaks: "My God, my God, why have you forsaken me?" This signifies the death of self because at this moment he's losing his personal relationship with God. He's losing his personal relationship with God because he's losing that which *has* a personal relationship with God—namely, self. Self is what has a personal relationship with God.

Now, self is not an easy thing to define. Ego is easy—it's the whole host of conditioned views, opinions, and distorted perceptions—but self is something different. If you think of self as a verb, you can see that it's something that happens within consciousness. Self is the act of consciousness turning back upon itself and reflecting within. That self-reflection is what self *is*. Self is not a thing; it's literally the act of consciousness turning back and looking within. Now, when one is very unified within, then there's no friction and no conflict, and what we experience inside is a great sense of peace and ease and well-being. In other words, there is nothing at odds within yourself or between you and the world, and everything is at peace. What the arc of consciousness turns and reflects upon inside is a deep state of peacefulness and ease and radiance.

But at some point in our spiritual evolution, that arc of self stops turning to look within. Why it stops turning is a hard thing to explain; that cessation is a form of maturity, the ultimate spiritual growing up. When consciousness stops turning in to reflect, all of a sudden there's no sense of a personal self, because the personal self *is* what self looks at. In an advanced state of spiritual development, what our self *is* is that state of peace and rest and ease, that radiance of consciousness. It's a very elevated sense of our own *being*. But when consciousness stops turning and looking within and reflecting upon the peaceful center, then the sense of self disappears all together. Then we've moved beyond identity all together.

In a certain sense, the whole process of awakening is going toward a truer and truer and truer identity. It starts with our awakening from ego to divine *being*—that's a shift of identity. And then our experience of divine *being* gets more unified, simpler and quieter, and our sense of who we are and what we are changes as our essence of divine *being* gets clearer and clearer. Ultimately, we reach a point when we are ready to let go even of that beautiful, subtle sense of self. It's like stepping off a cliff, because it's such a radical departure when self suddenly disappears, when consciousness turning and looking in disappears. From the moment when consciousness stops turning back on itself, there is no more personal sense of self or a personal relationship with God.

It's important to understand that I'm not talking philosophically, I'm not talking psychologically, and I'm not talking theologically. What I'm describing is experiential; there's nothing abstract about it. It's not something you believe in or don't believe in; instead it's something you've either experienced or you haven't experienced. As we've seen, Jesus' life embodies the spiritual journey, and in those last moments on the cross, he experiences the culmination of that journey. Because the dropping away of self is experienced as the ultimate death, it's really felt as a tremendous loss. The loss of self is not like transcending the ego. The ego is painful and conflicted, and it's a relief to leave it behind, but by the time self begins to fall away, your sense of yourself is radiant. What you're losing, then, is really the most beautiful thing you've ever experienced, the most beautiful thing you've ever known.

After the transfiguration, your connection with God is so deep it feels as if you're merged, and there's no sense of separation between you and God. To have that intimacy suddenly disappear is an immense transition, and this is graphically portrayed in the crucifixion. There's a sense, initially, of loss, because when you lose a personal self, you lose the personal God as well. For those who have come along a spiritual path focused on engendering a more intimate relationship with God, this can be a tremendous loss, because you've put all of your being into having a profound intimate relationship with God or with a deity. To have that fall away is shocking, to say the least.

And so Jesus is horrified at this: *My God, my God, why have you forsaken me?* He's lost his personal God; he's lost his personal self. *And Jesus uttered a loud cry and breathed his last.* Imagine what it would feel like to be forsaken; to scream out a loud, guttural cry; and then breathe your last breath, finally just letting it all go. In that last breath, Jesus lets his entire life go—even his relationship with God.

In the Gospel of Mark, this is the end of Jesus' life. It's an amazing ending because it doesn't leave everything tied up or tell you exactly what everything means. It certainly isn't a Hollywood ending.

The tragic death of Jesus depicted in Mark was a profound dilemma for the early Christian community. This was not what was supposed to happen to the Messiah predicted in the Jewish scriptures. That Messiah was to be a ruler here on earth who would usher in a new age of peace for the Jewish people. But Jesus said, "my Kingdom is not of the earth." And now his life ends not in triumph, but in tragedy. What are his disciples and early followers to make of this unthinkable ending?

The Gospel of Mark is uncompromising in its stark portrayal of the life and death of Jesus. Mark is a master of making his readers face what they would rather not face. His rendering of the Jesus story is not for the faint of heart, nor for those who want a romanticized version of spirituality. And yet his story is the gospel, meaning good news. So where is the good news in this tragic ending of the Jesus story as told by Mark?

There are many types of death. There is the peaceful death at the end of a long and happy life well lived. This is the death most people would prefer, though few will attain. There is the life-numbing death of addiction and denial. There is the death of succumbing to the world's harsh need to conform to its insanity and forsaking the life you could have lived had you only lived from the dictates of your own heart. Indeed, there are many types of death, but what we are not told is that most of them occur while we are living.

But Mark tells us, over and over again, that true life is not the life of the ego with all of its neurotic fears and desire for control and security. True life is life lived from the vitality of spirit, and the gospel is good news because, for Mark, Jesus opens the doorway to the Kingdom of Heaven here and now for all who have eyes to see and the courage to repent (to turn around, turn within) and receive the radiance of their true *being*.

Jesus must die, you see, because his life and death are the embodiment of the journey of spiritual awakening and liberation. And there is no liberation without the death of self, not physically but spiritually. You must die before you die so that you can be resurrected as the radiance of divine *being*. The original ending of Mark's gospel has no resurrection, only the suggestion of it earlier in the text. We, the reader, are left to be resurrected ourselves. But we can only be resurrected if we have taken the journey within ourselves that Jesus embodies in his life story.

The crucifixion embodies the death of self, and self is not an easy thing to define. When the ego is transcended (though rarely destroyed) at the moment of spiritual awakening, and you have gone through innumerable trials to burn away any remaining egoic resistance to spirit, you eventually come to the immovable peace of the transfigured state. In this state, self and God are indistinguishable from each other, and there is an ever-abiding experience of union and oneness with all beings.

The death of self that Jesus graphically embodies in the crucifixion is the falling away of the transfigured state of union with

God. When self falls away, any personal relationship with God falls away with it because all relationship only happens within the context of self. When we talk of *my* thoughts, or *my* feelings, or *my* opinions, we are essentially talking about a me that is in relationship with one's perception and experience. This split-mindedness is what self is. Self is the act of consciousness turning back upon itself, and relating to whatever it finds as self. We typically call this self-consciousness. In the transfigured state what we find when we look within is peace, union and oneness. With the falling away, or death of self, embodied in the crucifixion, all of this falls away. And when it does, it can initially feel like you are falling into an egoless, Godless, selfless void of nothingness.

What cannot be fully understood at the moment of the falling away of self is that what you are losing is your inner life. This is an extremely difficult thing to describe in anything other than negative terms, and yet with the falling away of self, there arises, or resurrects, a whole new life.

To most people to have no inner life is inconceivable, and yet it is simply the absence of consciousness reflecting upon the constant narration of the mind. What's left is a seamless flow of unity experienced not by a self, but by the unity itself. As the fourteenth century German mystic Meister Eckhart said, "The eye through which I see God is the same eye through which God sees me; my eye and God's eye are one eye, one seeing, one knowing, one love."

JESUS AND THE CRIMINALS

The crucifixion scene in the Gospel of Luke contains elements not found in Mark. Among them is the image of Jesus being crucified between two criminals who are themselves being crucified. In the Gospel of Luke it's written:

> Two others, who were criminals, were led away to be put
> to death with him. And when they came to the place
> that is called The Skull, there they crucified him, and
> the criminals, one on his right and one on his left. And
> Jesus said, "Father, forgive them, for they know not what
> they do." [Luke 23:32–34, ESV]

So imagine, you're nailed to a cross, which is a very painful way to go. In crucifixion, though your hands and feet are pierced with nails, you don't die from your injuries. As you hang on the cross, your body over many hours begins to weaken until you can no longer hold yourself upright. As your body weight begins to pull you down, it collapses your chest cavity and pushes the air out of your lungs. You eventually die of asphyxiation because your lungs can no longer provide oxygen for your body. It is a terrible, terrible way to go.

Imagine yourself in that situation with a criminal on your right and a criminal on your left. Metaphorically, these two criminals stand for the world of duality, and Jesus is the still point of eternity around which the dualistic world of time and space turns. The dualistic world is the world of good and bad and right and wrong, and Jesus is right there in the middle, between those dualities. The story continues:

> One of the criminals who were hanged railed at him,
> saying, "Are you not the Christ? Save yourself and
> us!" But the other rebuked him, saying, "Do you
> not fear God, since you are under the same sentence
> of condemnation? And we indeed justly, for we are
> receiving the due reward of our deeds; but this man has
> done nothing wrong." And he said, "Jesus, remember
> me when you come into your kingdom." And he said to

him, "Truly, I say to you, today you will be with me in
Paradise." [Luke 23:39–43, ESV]

One criminal is saying to Jesus, "If you're so great, if you're the
Christ, save us, perform a miracle, get us out of this!" He is operating from ego and so has closed himself off from salvation. The
other criminal, the one with the open heart who recognizes Jesus as
the Christ, knows they've done wrong and are receiving their just
reward. So there they are, Jesus and the criminals, each hanging
from a cross, dying, and the one with the open heart reaches out to
Jesus. He's one of the people who come into Jesus' life over and over
again during the gospel story, who recognize who Jesus is and what
he represents. From that recognition he asks Jesus, "Remember me
when you come into your kingdom."

The capacity to recognize divinity when you see it is the all-
important element. It's found in all the healing stories, and it's
what allows a few people to truly reach out to Jesus and to understand him. This criminal, at the end of his life, recognizes the
divinity right beside him. And that capacity to open to and recognize what's there—*that* is the saving grace. And Jesus says to
him, "Truly, I say to you, today you will be with me in Paradise."

When people recognize who and what Jesus is and have faith
in him, it mirrors back something important about our spiritual
journey. This is all about an internal journey, about your capacity
to recognize divinity whenever and wherever you encounter it. It
requires a certain sort of humility that allows you to peer beyond
the world of appearances and touch upon that spark of the timeless radiance. Whether you understand it or can do anything with
it doesn't matter in the slightest; all that matters is your capacity
to recognize that spark when you see it and to open yourself
in humility to its redeeming Grace. This is the magic of Jesus'
life. This is the miracle that surpasses all the other miracles—the

ability that Jesus has to mirror back divinity for those who are in his presence. This miracle is far superior to being able to walk on water or turn water into wine. It is the miracle of redemption, which awakens people to their own true nature.

THE DEATH OF JESUS IN THE GOSPEL OF JOHN

We've looked closely at how Jesus' life ends in the Gospel of Mark; now I want to contrast that with how his life ends in the Gospel of John. John has a very different view of Jesus. John views Jesus as the ultimate spiritual principle. From the Gospel of John we get those amazing "I am" statements, such as "I am the way, and the truth, and the life," [John 14:6, ESV] and "I am the light of the world" [John 8:12, NIV, ESV].

John has reconfigured the very human character of Jesus found in Mark into an abstract spiritual principle to such an extent that, at the beginning of the Gospel of John, Jesus usurps the Old Testament creation story in Genesis.

> In the beginning was the Word, and the Word was with God, and the Word was God. He was in the beginning with God. All things were made through him, and without him was not anything made that was made. In him was life, and the life was the light of men. [John 1:1–4, ESV]

In the Old Testament, God is the creator of heaven and earth. In the Gospel of John, Jesus is the creative principle. So John's Jesus is not like the Jesus we find in Mark. In the Gospel of Mark, we find a Jesus who, through living out his life, maps out the path of spiritual awakening to ultimate liberation. In the Gospel of John, Jesus is magisterial; he is in complete control of himself. It almost seems as though he's hovering above the events of the story, completely and totally unaffected. In the Gospel of John, Jesus is fully liberated from the very beginning. In a sense, John's portrayal of Jesus is the resurrected Jesus that continues where the Gospel of Mark leaves off. It's as if John understood the resurrected state alluded to, but not developed in Mark's Gospel, and rewrote the story from that perspective. So, in John we have a very different portrayal of Jesus—and thus, a very different portrayal of Jesus' death on the cross.

In John, the crucifixion opens with this scene:

> [S]tanding by the cross of Jesus were his mother and
> his mother's sister, Mary the wife of Clopas, and Mary
> Magdalene. When Jesus saw his mother and the disciple
> whom he loved standing nearby, he said to his mother,
> "Woman, behold, your son!" Then he said to the disciple,
> "Behold, your mother!" And from that hour the disciple
> took her to his own home. [John 19:25–27, ESV]

So standing at the cross are these three women and the beloved disciple, who is John, the gospel writer. John and Jesus have always had a tremendously close and intimate relationship. John has an instinct about how to be in right relationship with Jesus; he doesn't struggle, he doesn't strain, he has an intuitive way of knowing how to relate to divinity in just the right way. There, at the end of Jesus' life, all the disciples but John have abandoned him.

I've always found it very important that it was the three women who were there at the foot of his cross holding vigil. They didn't get scared, and they didn't abandon him. There's something very important about the feminine energy here. In a mythic sense, male energy is often portrayed as big and strong and fearless and courageous, but underneath that pretense and bluster, there is a weakness. Often times when we're pretending to be fearless or to be courageous, we pretend because deep inside we actually are afraid. Deep inside, we've touched upon a sense of insecurity, so we fake it, and try to look courageous or fearless. Feminine energy has a very different dynamic. Feminine energy is very connected with the world. Women are the life givers; every human being on the entire earth took form within the womb of a woman and was birthed from a woman. So the feminine perspective is connected with the earth, with something rich and grounded and nourishing. Above all else, the feminine is connected with a deep and profound love—a love that is its own courage, its own fearlessness. It has no bluster because it's real, rooted right into the soil of *being* itself. And so these three important women in Jesus' life have not abandoned him. There they are, standing vigil, caring for him to the last breath of his life.

And from the cross, Jesus now does something very beautiful. He says to his beloved disciple, "Now I entrust my mother to you, she is now your mother." It's a touching and beautiful act. Imagine that, as you're dying, one of your last acts is to unite two of the people that are closest and most important to you. You entrust them to each other, to take care of and watch out for each other.

To me this shows the love that really underlies Jesus' entire message. All of his decisive actions, miracles, healings, and condemnations of the religious political authorities were really fuelled by and grounded in a very deep love for humanity. After all, he dedicated his entire life to humanity. As the theology goes, "God so loved the world that he gave his only begotten son." That giving is an act of love and so Jesus' life was actually an embodiment of love. And here at the end, it all culminates in this very intimate and close union of his beloved disciple and his mother, as he entrusts them to each other. It's a very beautiful scene.

> After this, Jesus, knowing that all was now finished, said
> (to fulfill the Scripture), "I thirst." A jar full of sour wine
> stood there, so they put a sponge full of the sour wine on
> a hyssop branch and held it to his mouth. When Jesus
> had received the sour wine, he said, "It is finished," and he
> bowed his head and gave up his spirit. [John 19:28–30, ESV]

The ending of Jesus' life in John is completely different than in Mark. In Mark, Jesus' last breath was a loud death cry from exhaustion and torment. In the Gospel of John, Jesus right to the very end maintains his dignity and balance, and remains centered in divine *being*. With his last breath, Jesus simply says, "It is finished." Jesus has lived out his destiny; he's played his part well, and he has no regrets. I think anyone would hope to have this feeling at the end of their life—that they'd lived their life well, that they'd given *all* of themselves to their incarnation, that they'd lavishly poured forth their truth and their love and their light upon the world, holding nothing back. Then, the end of life holds no regrets, simply the feeling Jesus had: "It is finished." What a beautiful way to end the life of Jesus.

THE RESURRECTION 14

> Christ has no body now on earth but yours.
>
> ST. THERESA OF AVILA

The final scene in the Jesus story is the resurrection. As we've seen, with many of the key scenes in the life of Jesus, each of the gospel writers has a different viewpoint, and that's true of the resurrection as well. I want to look at the resurrection as Mark depicts it.

THE MYSTERY OF THE RESURRECTION

The Gospel of Mark contains a very short description of the resurrection, one with a rather abrupt ending. Though the text does continue with stories about Jesus meeting with his disciples after he arises, this material—from Mark 16:9 onward—is considered a later addition intended to explain the original version of the resurrection as Mark depicted it. I believe this additional material lessens the impact, so I'm going to stick with the original version as Mark wrote it.

Jesus has been taken down from the cross and buried in a cave, and a large stone has been rolled in front of the cave so no one can enter. And then Mary Magdalene, Mary the mother of James, and Salome show up. This is how Mark depicts this scene:

> When the Sabbath was past, Mary Magdalene, Mary the mother of James, and Salome bought spices, so that they might go and anoint him. And very early on the first day of the week, when the sun had risen, they went to the tomb. And they were saying to one another, "Who will roll away the stone for us from the entrance of the tomb?" And looking up, they saw that the stone had been rolled back—it was very large. And entering the tomb, they saw a young man sitting on the right side, dressed in a white robe, and they were alarmed. And he said to them, "Do not be alarmed. You seek Jesus of Nazareth, who was crucified. He has risen; he is not here. See the place where they laid him. But go, tell his disciples and Peter that he is going before you to Galilee. There you will see him, just as he told you." And they went out and fled from the tomb, for trembling and astonishment had seized them, and they said nothing to anyone, for they were afraid. [Mark 16:1–8, ESV]

This is how the resurrection ends in Mark. It's a very brief, very intense scene. Mary Magdalene and Mary, the mother of James, and Salome return to the cave where Jesus was entombed. An immense stone had been rolled in front of the cave entrance, so they're wondering how they will move the stone in order to anoint him with oils and spice. You can imagine their astonishment when they get to the tomb and discover that this great boulder has been rolled away from the mouth of the cave. Who did it? How had they done it? The stone was much too heavy for one person to move.

Their second surprise was to find this young man, clothed all in white, sitting quite peacefully, quite tranquilly inside the tomb. We don't know who he is; Mark never says who he is. This same man—or perhaps angelic being—is found on the periphery of some earlier scenes in the story. In Mark's description of Jesus' arrest in the Garden of Gethsemane, there is also a mention of this man clothed in white who runs away, but he isn't identified. There's much speculation among scholars about who he might have been, but I think it's left ambiguous for a reason. This mystery adds to the dramatic flair of the story—and after all, this story is the unfolding of a spiritual mystery.

Now, these three women are deeply rooted in a compassionate, openhearted femininity. They've come as an act of love and devotion to anoint Jesus' body with oil and spices. Even though he's dead, they remain devoted; they haven't abandoned him, as his disciples did. Entering the tomb, they meet this strange young man clothed in white, and he assures them that everything is perfectly fine. He tells them Jesus has risen and gone to Galilee, and he instructs them to tell his disciples.

You can imagine the shock they must have felt. First the giant boulder is moved, and then in the empty tomb—where they didn't expect to find anything inside but the body of Jesus— they encounter this young man clothed in white, almost like an angel, sitting there beatific, calm, and unafraid. It's a shocking moment, and these three women are astonished and afraid. They flee from the tomb, trembling with fear.

Jesus' absence is miraculous, but it's miraculous in a terrifying way; they don't know exactly what has happened. The mysterious man alludes to the resurrection. He says that Jesus will meet the disciples in Galilee, and the other gospel writers will take up this theme and add many stories about Jesus and the disciples after the resurrection. But in Mark we get the shortest, most intense version.

Of course, Mark always goes for the surprise; he turns corners in his storytelling that you don't expect, and this is the beauty of Mark. Mark doesn't always read eloquently; he's not a poet like the writer of John's gospel. He's more interested in exploring the unexpected shifts and turns of the story, and I think he does this because it opens the mind and heart to the mysteriousness of life. When we keep reading things that are unexpected and encountering scenes that sometimes end almost before they've begun, it leaves us in a mysterious state of *being*. And I think this state of openness is where the writer of the Gospel of Mark wanted to leave us. This is the state in which we can recognize the radiance, and when we're open and caught off guard by the winds of spirit, we can be transformed into its shining.

As the Bible says of spirit, it comes like a thief in the night, when you least expect it. Mark's gospel is literally constructed to put you in these moments of strange turns of scene that abruptly end without an ending. But if you really embody the story, if you really let yourself go into the story, then you too may come into that state of openness. You too may come into that place where time stops and the spinning world aligns with eternity. From that state you can open to your own presence of *being*, the divine *being* that we all are.

LIFE AFTER RESURRECTION

There are other reasons why the resurrection is such an interesting part of the Jesus story. While the theme of resurrection is an ancient one, Jesus' resurrection and what it means have no exact parallel in spiritual literature—especially in contrast to many forms of Eastern spirituality, where the whole idea is to awaken from the world of time and space, to get off the wheel of karma, to arrive at a state of spiritual enlightenment so you will no longer be reincarnated. The goal in these forms of spirituality is literally to leap off of the wheel of the dualistic world and transcend it, so you don't have to come back into form.

Jesus' story is just the opposite. Jesus descends directly from the Kingdom of Heaven; he descends from enlightenment into the human condition. This signifies a way that spirit, rather than trying to escape the dualistic world that we live in, is *giving* itself to the world. Spirit is relinquishing itself, out of love, back into the world, to bring forth the light of radiance into the world and reveal that nothing is separated from divinity; nothing is actually other than the divine itself.

We find the same emphasis on embodied spirit at the very end of the Jesus story. Jesus' life ends on the cross; that death is the great release, the great transcendence of time and space. But of course, his life doesn't really end with the crucifixion; it culminates in the resurrection, as once again Jesus comes back to the world of time and space. In the journey of awakening, when self has been annihilated and dropped away, we experience a kind of resurrection. We realize a new orientation. In other words, we are no longer the center of our individual lives, and life is no longer about satisfying oneself, not even in order to arrive at some spiritual state of development.

I'm not saying that there is no more spiritual development beyond, but that the self-oriented life is over. That is what has died. The resurrection depicts what comes after that—after the destiny of one's personal story is lived out, yet there's still a life to live. This is where the resurrection provides a mirror that something does come back; something survives the death of self. Now, in the Gospel of Mark it isn't made clear exactly what survives, what actually resurrects. Individually, what comes back to life out of the ashes of the death of self is something that's really quite simple, but quite poignant. From that place, the only thing left to do is to be a benevolent presence in the world. I don't say this because one wants to do it or tries to do it. All attempts to be spiritual or pure or compassionate or loving, all of that striving is just what the ego or self tries to do or to be. But when all that falls away, there's literally nothing left to do; there's no life orientation that makes sense other than to be a selfless and benevolent presence. This may happen on a big stage, but it may just mean being a benevolent grandmother or a mother or daughter or son or business owner. It doesn't have to look any particular way, and in fact the resurrected state can actually look quite normal.

Of course, when we look at the life of Jesus, we get the impression that the spiritually awakened state always looks impressive and charismatic, but that's just what makes good storytelling. The resurrection within oneself is something far quieter. When self is annihilated, there is often a temporary sense of living in ashes, living among the dead. The new orientation isn't immediately or intuitively recognized. In the same way, when you were a baby, you had an innate capacity to walk and later to run but didn't yet have the capability developed. You didn't really know how to do it; you had to stand up on your feet and take a step and fall down and get up and take another step. Even though you were born with innate capacities—to walk, to run, to use language—each capacity doesn't immediately come online. We have to orient ourselves around them and develop into them. Our capacities are there in potential but take a little while to come into bloom.

Part of the resurrection occurs when what is left in the wake of the crucifixion opens its eyes and discovers that everything it ever thought itself to be—not only ego, but all the spiritual experiences and definitions—is dead. It's not immediately clear what life is going to look like. One's whole sense of passion and of drive belongs to the self, to the ego, even when it's very positive or for the benefit of all beings. It's very hard to convey what moves you when all of that is gone. It comes from a place that is very, very simple. In the Zen tradition, they say, when you're hungry you eat, and when you're tired you sleep. That doesn't sound very exciting, but it's pointing to the simplicity of a life no longer driven by the inner forces of desire and aversion—by wanting to accomplish, or to escape, or even to convey something.

What remains is a great heartfulness, a great sense of compassion for the world. Even though the word *resurrection* implies a rising, it's not as if we rise above everything and everyone. Resurrection is the rising from the death of self, but there's no hierarchy in it. There's no sense of being better than, or nobler than, or more elevated than anyone else—all of that belongs to ego and self. There's just a simple, profound intimacy with all things, and with all beings, and with that which transcends all things and all beings. Life is experienced in all of its original completeness and unity.

That intimacy *is* the resurrected state. We see that all that we perceive is actually our own *being*. I recall one Zen master saying, "My true personality includes the entire universe." That's a big statement, and if that were said from the ego, it would point to a frightening self-inflation. What this saying really conveys is an intimate way of experiencing each moment in all of its completeness and divinity.

When Jesus appears, he's not immediately recognized; people don't really know or trust who he really is—including some of the disciples. All this is just part of the storytelling, an attempt to convey what it is to live from a state of *being* that's not of the world of time and space. As Jesus said, "I'm in the world, but not *of* it." I think this is the best possible description of the resurrection: to have an absolute intimacy with the world of time and space and things and people and events—but not be *of* the world. You are *of* the world of eternity, the Kingdom of Heaven.

THREE

DISCIPLES OF THE ETERNAL

ARCHETYPES OF THE JESUS STORY

15

> If a man is to live, he must be all alive,
> body, soul, mind, heart, spirit.
>
> **THOMAS MERTON**

Thus far, I've interpreted the story of Jesus through the lens of the perennial spiritual journey to full awakening, which by its very nature is revolutionary. I've interpreted each of the scenes within the story as representations of stages of the spiritual journey as well as a mirror to certain realities within us—namely the reality of divine *being*. But the character and life of Jesus is so extraordinary and otherworldly that his story alone doesn't necessarily teach us how to *engage* in that awakening journey.

EMBODIED DIVINITY

The goal here is to embody the entire story, to embody spirit in human form—not just the transcendent moments, but also the darkness and doubt and betrayal. To do this, we have to relate not only to Jesus, but also to the other key characters in the Gospels—Peter, John, Judas, Pontius Pilate, and Mary Magdalene. These five characters, in the way each relates to Jesus, embody five different archetypal ways of relating with spirit and with the spiritual impulse within us. We can internalize these characters and their energies in the same way that we internalize the stages of the awakening journey in Jesus' life.

Our tendency, when we read any story, is to identify with the noble, heroic characters, so it goes against our natural inclination to identify with Judas or with Pontius Pilate. We all want to understand and relate to the Jesus part of the story—the light, glory, beauty, truth, and transcendence that he represents. But these five figures represent the darker, more shadowy parts of the psyche that we don't readily embrace or even want to admit are present.

We're dealing with the language of myth, so many of the key players in the story are overstated, made larger than life in order to highlight certain archetypal traits. We're unlikely to find Judas's deep wound or Peter's overconfidence in quite the same form within ourselves, although we might. But in the larger view, once we see that each of these characters can be seen sympathetically—because their actions stem from their own wounding or passion or sorrow or fear—then we can meet them with compassion. We can find them not only within ourselves, but reflected all around us in life. When we see that many of the people around us act the way they do out of pain, or suffering, or sorrow, we can meet them, as well as ourselves, with compassionate understanding.

These archetypes are universal and timeless. They're as true and as potent today as they were in Jesus' time. Take the story of Mary Magdalene: almost everyone can relate to her, because at some point in our lives we've all felt the need for redemption, felt lost and broken, or done something we felt was unforgivable. But it's through brokenness that the redemption comes—and that's why it's so important that we embody these characters and find them within ourselves.

The Jesus story gives us an example of how embodied spirit moves in the world, but these five archetypal figures give us the emotional and energetic connection to both the light and dark sides of the psyche that we have to understand and contend with so that spirit starts to awaken and move within us.

Each of these characters has a core flaw or wound that defines their character. Seeing these parts of ourselves—parts we don't want to acknowledge—can be humbling. But it's through our humility that spirit connects to and infuses our humanity. Before we can fully embody spirit, we need to see what in us is resisting spirit. We need to encounter these archetypal forces within ourselves.

THE ARCHETYPE OF PETER

Peter is one of the central characters in the Jesus story. He meets Jesus and is inspired by his radiant and powerful charisma. In fact, he's completely taken by the presence of Jesus; he uproots himself from his life and becomes one of Jesus' early disciples. The character of Peter represents, in part, that place within each of us that comes alive when we come into contact with someone that deeply inspires us, when we sense a deep level of truthfulness and vitality in another. Peter comes alive in the presence of divine *being* in the form of Jesus and immediately became one of his followers.

Peter's character is one of the most interesting archetypal characters in the whole story of Jesus. As we've seen, Peter always misses the mark. He stands for that way of *being* that never quite gets it right. If sin is to miss the mark as a kind of innocent mistake, then Peter represents that innocent mistake; he never quite responds to the moment in the way that the moment dictates. Peter is well intentioned and enthusiastic to the point of over-confidence. He overestimates himself at almost every point in the story. He's so certain that he doesn't have any human frailty, that he won't fail, that he won't turn away from Jesus, yet everything that Peter says he won't do, he ends up doing.

Now, part of this overconfidence is a veiling for what really drives Peter's life—and what really drives Peter's life is fear. This is part of the make-up of the human psyche. Sometimes when you experience fear, you overcompensate and try to appear more confident and more certain than you really are. At the beginning, the fear doesn't really get in Peter's way. He makes a leap that very few people would take, and immediately becomes a follower and disciple of Jesus, leaving his known life behind. He appears at first to be not only an inspired man, but a courageous man. But we'll come to see as the story unfolds that Peter is constantly overestimating himself, and his capabilities and personality traits stem from his underlying nature, which is fear.

At the most crucial moments, Peter is seized by fear—or by its compensating emotion, overconfidence. The entire Jesus story is marked by vital moments in which the decisions that are made and the way that various characters respond have real consequences. All of our lives have such vital moments, but often it's only in retrospect that we realize how important they were.

Now, at one point in the story, Jesus has a foretelling of the future that he shares with his disciples. Jesus has realized that at some point they're all going to abandon him, that they're all going to deny him. Overconfident Peter stands up and says, "I will never deny you." And of course, Jesus knows Peter is going to deny him, but what can he say? There is Peter, exercising his nature. He overestimates himself because he lacks the essential grounding in humility that would keep him connected to his heart, connected to the deeper realities of his character. But because Peter's viewpoint is based in fear, he doesn't want to see this. He wants to run from his weakness, and he wants Jesus to make everything right in his life.

And of course, it doesn't happen that way. At the Last Supper, when all the disciples are together, Jesus says, "Before the cock crows twice you will deny me three times." Jesus knows Peter's character; he understands Peter better than Peter understands himself. Once again Peter argues that he won't deny Jesus, and once again Peter is overestimating himself.

I think that if we really look inside, we can find a little bit of Peter's character in ourselves. It grows out of that little seed of fear at the center of our *being*. Our desire is to cover over that fear, to find some other compensating emotion or compensating orientation to life, so we don't have to deal with it or encounter it directly. Different people have different ways of dealing with the fear. Some will shrink away from the fear, while others, like Peter, will rise up with false bravado.

As you remember, Peter is actually the first to deny Jesus. The young girl in the courtyard identifies him as a disciple of Jesus, and Peter denies ever knowing Jesus. She accuses him three times, and Peter denies Jesus three times in quick succession. Thus, the prophecy comes true.

Over and over again, Peter misses the mark at the most crucial moments. His dilemma is not simply that he's trying to compensate for his fear, but that he's not honest with himself. He doesn't want to see his human frailty; he doesn't want to encounter his fallibility. But in our lives—and especially in our spiritual lives—it's absolutely essential that we develop a state of real honesty. This is what humility is all about. We need not feel humiliated by our human nature, with all its strengths and weaknesses; but if we're really honest, we'll be humbled by it, because, for all of us, there is a frailty to our human nature. There's our obvious physical frailty—we can all get sick, we can all have accidents, and we will certainly all die—but there are also emotional frailties deep inside that we would like to pretend aren't there.

Peter is the archetype for a particular human frailty; he doesn't quite have the honesty to face himself. If Peter could face himself, if he could own up to his own human weaknesses, then he might be able to move beyond them. But he can't admit them; he's in a constant state of denying them, and therefore, he overestimates himself at each moment and continues to miss the mark. Good intentions don't really count for much if we can't be entirely honest with ourselves. The archetypal character of Peter reminds us all of the need to look honestly at our own frailties.

THE ARCHETYPE OF JUDAS

Besides Jesus himself, Judas is the most iconic of all the gospel characters. Judas has come down through history as a malicious, evil figure. After all, he's the one to ultimately blame for Jesus' death, because he turned Jesus in. Judas is, at the end of the day, a very unlikable character.

As I have already mentioned, there are many different ways of interpreting the character of Judas. But if we look at Judas through the most common interpretive lens of evil, we can begin to have a deeper understanding of this darkest aspect of the human psyche. The archetype of Judas is that dark aspect of the wounded psyche that strikes out at what it loves. Judas is attracted to divine *being*, but because of some deep wound hidden at the core of his psyche, he has a deep cynicism and distrust of the very thing he seeks. Through the course of the story, Judas's cynicism and distrust will transform into a malicious evil that strikes out at the very thing he loves: Jesus.

Judas is a tortured soul who had hoped that Jesus could save him from his own darkness, but he cannot allow in Jesus' saving grace because he cannot, or will not, face himself. He is resistant to the transformation he seeks. He wants to become as Jesus is, but he cannot. And since he cannot become what he loves, he must destroy it.

But at the beginning, Judas is inspired by Jesus. He has the capacity—as many people do not—to notice something extraordinary when he sees it. When he meets Jesus, his presence lights up something in Judas's own personality. So clearly, Judas had the capacity to recognize this deeper reality that Jesus represents. He had the capacity to see or feel or intuit beyond the appearance of things, to the divine light that shines through. That's why he was attracted to Jesus in the first place. So Judas represents that which is at once drawn to the light and simultaneously repelled by it—not only out of fear, but also out of self-destructiveness. We have no way of knowing whether some event in his life turned something at the deepest core of his being to darkness and shadow or whether he was simply born that way, but either way, he carries a deep sense of lack within himself.

Now, this sense of lack is not unusual. In fact, to feel that there's something essentially wrong with oneself is one of the core sicknesses of Western culture. The whole of Western culture is rooted in the sense there's something essentially wrong with oneself, and this comes in from our religious traditions. From Genesis, we've received the message that to exist as a human being is to exist in a fallen state of sin. So the theology that has defined

Western culture is that there's something essentially wrong with you, that your existence is somehow essentially flawed.

Now, I don't think that any human being's existence—or *any* existence at all—is a mistake. However, there is a common feeling many people have that something's not quite right. It could be something about you, or it could be something about the world at large, but something's not quite right. That feeling gives rise to a sense of disconnectedness and separation. As long as we're in the egoic realm of consciousness, we feel isolated, because we think and therefore feel that we are contained within the confines of our own skin and bones, which defines a very marked line of separation between us and everything and everybody else, including God. This perspective of separation gives rise to a sense of alienation. When we feel separate, when we feel alienated, what starts to grow from that perspective is a sense of wrongness: that *there's something essentially wrong with me.*

As I said, in Western culture almost everybody you ever bump into will feel that something is essentially not quite right; they have what in modern language we'd call a bad self-image. Judas is an archetype for the feeling that there's something not quite right blown up to malicious proportions. He's the personification of a kind of evil darkness at the core of *being* that he is not even aware of.

This sense that there's something wrong is universal. In Buddhism, they call it Maya, or illusion. Maya, in Buddhist theology, weaves a veil of illusion that makes you *feel* and *think* there's separation where there really isn't any; it's a kind of cosmic mistake. But in our Western religions, illusion isn't an innocent mistake. It becomes something dark and evil. In the religions that shaped Western culture, we've mythologized the sense of existential lack and personified it as the devil. What the East sees as essentially an innocent mistake, we see as evil.

Judas *hopes* that the presence of Jesus, the charisma of this powerful spiritual figure, will finally fill him up and make him whole. But as the story unfolds, it's clear that nothing can really fill Judas up. Judas is like what Buddhism calls a hungry ghost; no matter how much he takes in, he has a bottomless stomach, an inner void that he feels can't be filled by anything.

This is a very human response, to try to fill up the inner sense of lack. But nothing that we ever try to fill it up with will fill it, until we can actually go within and encounter it directly. When that lack can be encountered directly and there can be a sense of love and compassion and sympathy for that experience, then that wound can be healed—but until then, no amount of goodness, no amount of holiness, no amount of charisma from the outside can ever make us feel whole. No amount of love will ever fill that feeling of emptiness. It is all an illusion of course, but illusions feed off of our denial of them.

In the character of Judas, this emptiness just gnaws away at him, and he becomes more and more malicious as the story goes on. Finally, at the Last Supper, the climactic moment of Judas's life arrives. Jesus dips a piece of bread into wine, infusing it with the malicious presence of evil, and puts it into Judas's mouth. Now Judas's fate is sealed. His nature has been confirmed, and nothing will stop him from betraying his master—because, in its most malicious form, lack of self-worth lashes out at the very thing it loves most. It will try to destroy or to kill the very thing it wants most, and that's what Judas does. He's the one who turns Jesus in to the authorities; he's the one who points Jesus out by giving him a kiss. What a terrible and darkly intimate way to betray the one he loves.

Now, in mythological stories, *everything* is overblown. Everything is made big so that you cannot miss its significance. There's a long history of people wanting to see Judas as something *out there.* "I'm not Judas, I would never behave that way, I would never deny and try to destroy the very thing I love." But I think if we can enter into that place of humility and honesty within ourselves, each of us can find, in some measure, a little of what Judas represents.

Most people I meet in my teaching work do feel a certain existential lack. For some it comes as a result of a traumatic event, when they innocently turned their back on their own divinity, without knowing exactly what they were doing. Other people just seem to incarnate and come into the world with a sense that there's something not quite right about themselves. Still others experience it as they grow up and encounter the awkward dawning of self-consciousness. It isn't a comfortable kind of self-consciousness; it reminds you that you don't quite fit in. You begin to feel a sense of inauthenticity, and out of that inauthenticity grows a sense of lack that can be interpreted as "there's something essentially wrong with me."

All of this is, in the end, illusory. Still, it can be felt very deeply and very painfully. It's not until we can encounter this deep lack with a real sense of love and fearlessness that our old existential wounds can find their healing, allowing the various psychological forces within us to begin to come together and unify. Judas never seems quite able or willing to do this. His sense of lack runs rampant until it lashes out in an act of malicious betrayal.

It's possible to meet our sense of lack with great compassion for the sense of otherness and separation that it creates. The sense of lack is not in and of itself evil; it is simply the perceiving of separation where there is in fact only completeness and unity. It is a state of spiritual unconsciousness that Jesus is constantly trying to awaken people from. This is what spirituality is all about—finding out that we are whole, that we always have been whole. No matter how alienated anybody has ever felt, they've never actually been even a breath away from the divine. The true nature of all beings is divine *being* itself. But Judas stands for the ultimate form of forgetfulness and for what can arise out of inner anguish projected onto others.

As Jesus said from the cross about those who killed him, "Forgive them, for they know not what they do." This statement is a radical departure from the religion of his birth where man and woman make a terrible mistake and are cursed by God. It's also a radical departure from the Christian message transmitted by many of the churches today that teach that you are stained with original sin.

The message of Christian theology is often one of judgment, but that isn't the message that came from Jesus' mouth. He said, "Do not judge them, for they know not what they do. Forgive them. They've been blinded by their own misunderstanding." In other words, they haven't yet realized what Jesus realized: the fullness of divine *being*.

Jesus moved among the underclass—the sick, the outcasts, the ones who made mistakes. Those were the people he preached his message to. Those were the people he came to this earth for, and those were the people I believe he was speaking to at the very end of his life. *Forgive them, for they know not what they do.*

And who are those people? They're you and me. They're all of us. Nobody is perfect in this regard. Jesus is reminding us of the presence of divine *being* within us all. And Judas is reminding us of that within ourselves that wants the healing balm and craves the radiance of *being* and yet feels unworthy of it. That deep sense of lack and unworthiness that is epidemic in our culture has a hard time accepting the radiance of grace, because it's so contrary to how we see ourselves. That's Judas's dilemma, and it's not unlike the dilemma of most human beings. Judas's unworthiness turned into its most malignant and malicious form, but we can all find a little bit of what Judas suffered from.

THE ARCHETYPE OF PONTIUS PILATE

Pontius Pilate is similar to Judas in several ways. Pilate and Judas are two of the most misunderstood people in the entire Jesus story. Both characters are easy to dislike or even hate, but both show us something very important about human nature.

I am not looking strictly at the historical figure of Pontius Pilate here but rather at what he represents in the Jesus story, as well as what archetype of the human psyche he expresses. Pontius Pilate is an archetype for the rational leader. He is the Roman governor of Judea, and he's entrusted with keeping the peace and ensuring that the civil society runs smoothly. What he signifies is that part of each of us that acts from the rational mind to the exclusion of the heart. There can be, however, a certain amount of nobility in his rationality and a strong sense of commitment to his civic responsibilities.

You sense that Pilate sees himself as a good person, a moral person, and an ethical person. He gives Jesus a lot of time to explain himself. He doesn't just throw him to the crowd to be crucified simply to get on with it; he takes his time to delve into why the crowd is so intent on having this man killed.

The weak spot in Pontius Pilate's character is the same as his strength: his rationality. Rationality is a very useful capacity to have, but it is also a weakness because it keeps him from fully listening to his intuition. As he questions Jesus, he begins to relate to Jesus more and more, and we get the sense that he really comes to believe that Jesus is an innocent man—and not only an innocent man, but a good man.

In fact, though the story is ambiguous, it seems that Pontius Pilate may even believe that Jesus is an authentic spiritual figure. Maybe he *is* the King of the Jews; maybe he is the Savior and the Messiah. Pontius Pilate doesn't know, but the more he talks to Jesus, the more he gets the sense that this is an innocent man and a man of great stature.

Pilate's question to Jesus, "What is truth?" [John 18:38, NIV, ESV] has come down through the ages, and theologians have spent a lot of time examining the significance of his questioning Jesus. How often would a political leader and authority ask an accused criminal about truth? Simply by asking the question, Pilate shows that he has a certain amount of respect for Jesus—and perhaps a sense that this man before him knows something very, very important. It is as though Pilate himself is on the threshold of his own discovery about the truth that Jesus represents. He is, unlike so many of the religious authorities that Jesus encounters, genuinely curious as to exactly who Jesus is and what truth he preaches about.

So Pilate also stands for that place inside of us that really wants to know truth. Yet he's primarily interested in truth in the sense of *facts:* what did you do, when did you do it, and why does this mob want to crucify you? These are the kind of questions that Pilate is interested in; this is the way he thinks of truth. Now to Jesus, truth is something completely different. It's not about what happened and why it happened; it's not about facts. To Jesus, truth is a state of *being.* As he says, "My Kingdom is not of this world."

The truth that Jesus signifies is not the truth of history, or of facts, or of physics, or of mathematics or biology or the sciences, and it's certainly not the truth of political policy; it's eternal truth, the truth of *being.* Jesus' truth is the absolute truth of what we all are. That's what makes it divine, what brings it into the spiritual domain of eternity.

Jesus' truth intrigues Pontius Pilate, but it puts him in a bind. He has a crowd of angry people outside who want Jesus to be crucified; yet he feels that Jesus is an innocent man, perhaps an extraordinary man. How is he going to deal with this dilemma? What type of truth will he ultimately abide by? If he lets Jesus go, he's in trouble because the crowd will be enraged, and his number one priority as the governor of Judea is to keep the peace and, above all else, maintain order. This puts him in a moral bind: is he going to do what his instincts say is the right thing to do and let this man go, or is he going to do what his rational mind suggests and his political position dictates, which is to crucify Jesus, if for no other reason than to keep peace and order?

Historically, Pilate has often been seen as a terrible figure, as the man responsible for killing Jesus. In some of the other Gospels he is seen this way, but in the Gospel of John, Pilate seems a much more sympathetic character. If we really want to get a deep understanding of him, as with all these characters, we have to bring him very close to ourselves in order to find the human archetype that Pilate embodies.

Within each of us, we can find rationality in its best sense— that part of us that looks at the facts of a given situation and really tries to decide what's the right thing to do in order to fulfill our given role. There's a certain kind of ethical and moral compass that comes from doing this, but the weakness of pure rationality is that it doesn't give room to the heart, to one's deeper intuitions, to the innate sense of what is right or wrong beyond what the rational mind may appreciate or acknowledge. Sometimes our intuition is at odds with what our rational mind would say is necessary. People often find themselves in this dilemma. How do I understand what's really true? Is my rational mind going to tell me what's true, or is my intuitive sense going to tell me what's true? For most people, their intuition isn't always on the mark, so it's easy to be unclear when it comes to our intuition. For many people, intuition is a muscle that's not used enough to know when its coming from a true place of clarity and wisdom, or simply from emotion.

This is the dilemma that Pilate represents. He has a deep sense that Jesus is innocent. In the Gospel of John, he even says to the crowd, "I find no guilt in him," but they demand that Jesus be crucified. So Pilate's in a bind—damned if he does and damned if he doesn't. This shows us how Pilate is relating to his own spiritual impulse, to his own question, *What is truth?* His question about truth is ultimately a spiritual question, an existential question. It has to do with the truth of his existence: what he is, what life is, what God is, and what he is going to serve when it counts most.

The deep questions of existence break through the mundane order and open the door to the spiritual domain that underlies our entire life. And Pilate is right on the edge of stepping beyond the surface appearance of events and operating from a higher order of *being*. Is he going to ultimately be beholden to his political authority and its attendant responsibilities, bound by his rational nature, or is he going to open up to his intuitive nature, to that which tells him the truth about Jesus?

As we all know by now, in the end he gives Jesus over to be crucified. And yet he leaves a final hint when he writes "The King of the Jews" on the cross. When the Jews want him to change it so that it reads, "This man *said*, I am the King of the Jews," Pontius Pilate refuses, saying, "What I have written I have written." [John 19:20–22, ESV] It's as if he wanted the religious leaders to know that *he* thought that this was a man of significance. By this gesture, he's saying: this actually might be your Messiah, and look at what you're doing to him.

211

Pontius Pilate is an archetype for what people feel in their *being* in those moments of life when they have to decide: What's the most important thing? What do I really value most? What am I going to serve—the deep truth at the core of my *being* or the relative truth of the rational domain? What am I really going to orient my life around? And when those vital moments of decision come, what am I going to orient myself towards?

Ultimately, Pilate orients himself to his archetypal nature as the rational leader. But his dilemma makes each of us ask ourselves, what is *my* orientation at those critical moments, and will I act on my deeper intuitions come what may? What do I really value after all? Pilate embodies a question that we each must deal with in our life, because when we open to the spiritual dimension, we're opening to a trans-rational dimension of experience. Trans-rational means not that it's irrational and full of magical thinking, but that it comes from a wisdom and order of truth that's beyond the rational mind. What's going to orient us in our spiritual search and in our everyday lives?

So this question that Pilate is known for, "What is truth?" is really the fundamental question of our lives. Over and over this question comes back to us. It arises in big ways with the existential issues of life, when we ask ourselves what is the truth of our own *being*, the truth of life in general, and the truth of God. But it also arises in relative ways, in daily life. When you're having an argument, what's the *truth*? Being oriented toward the truth is different than being oriented toward being right or getting your way. Pontius Pilate stands for that question, what's the most important thing to you? What are you going to orient your life around? And when it really counts, when everything's on the line, what are you going to serve? From where does your action arise? Does it come from the truth center? Does it come from the rational center? Does it come from simply the chaotic nature of emotion? This is the mirror that the archetype of Pontius Pilate holds up to us.

THE ARCHETYPE OF MARY MAGDALENE

Mary Magdalene is the archetype for redemption. From the very beginning she's a very sympathetic figure. Her nature is simple; it is to love much. But Mary has lost her way in life, and her natural inclination to love much has been degraded into lust. Perhaps she is a prostitute, perhaps not; but she is "a sinner of the city," and an unwelcome guest at the Pharisees' dinner party where Jesus is the main guest.

Mary arrives on the scene unannounced and uninvited.

> One of the Pharisees asked him [Jesus] to eat with him, and he went into the Pharisee's house and reclined at the table. And behold, a woman of the city, who was a sinner, when she learned that he was reclining at table in the Pharisee's house, brought an alabaster flask of ointment, and standing behind him at his feet, weeping, she began to wet his feet with her tears and wiped them with the hair of her head and kissed his feet and anointed them with the ointment. [Luke 7: 36–38, ESV]

At this dinner party, Mary suddenly appears and immediately walks up to Jesus and breaks open a flask of very expensive perfume and begins lavishly pouring it over his body. Then she breaks down weeping, and before you know it she's at his feet, wiping her tears off his feet with her hair. It's a very powerful and poignant moment. The scene continues:

Now when the Pharisee who had invited him saw this, he said to himself, "If this man were a prophet, he would have known who and what sort of woman this is who is touching him, for she is a sinner." And Jesus answering said to him, "Simon, I have something to say to you." And he answered, "Say it, Teacher."

"A certain moneylender had two debtors. One owed five hundred denarii, and the other fifty. When they could not pay, he cancelled the debt of both. Now which of them will love him more?" Simon answered, "The one, I suppose, for whom he cancelled the larger debt." And he said to him, "You have judged rightly." Then turning toward the woman he said to Simon, "Do you see this woman? I entered your house; you gave me no water for my feet, but she has wet my feet with her tears and wiped them with her hair. You gave me no kiss, but from the time I came in she has not ceased to kiss my feet. You did not anoint my head with oil, but she has anointed my feet with ointment. Therefore I tell you, her sins, which are many, are forgiven—for she loved much. But he who is forgiven little, loves little." And he said to her, "Your sins are forgiven." Then those who were at table with him began to say among themselves, "Who is this, who even forgives sins?" And he said to the woman, "Your faith has saved you; go in peace." [Luke 7:39–50, ESV]

Mary's nature, as it says, is to love much. She has most likely lived her life as a prostitute, yet now she finds herself drawn to Jesus. This is a theme that plays out over and over in the Jesus story. There are people like Mary, often in a state of desperation or deep suffering, who somehow intuitively recognize the divine presence in Jesus. They're drawn to him magnetically because it's in the divine presence that their suffering finds its healing. At the moment when Mary encounters Jesus, she sees the degraded life she's lived, and she breaks down weeping with shame and falls at his feet. She is humbled; she is ashamed; she is humiliated. She takes her hair and wipes her tears from his feet. This is all her nature. Her nature is to love, and there's a beautifully vulnerable quality about her *being*. In the presence of Jesus, in the presence of divine *being*, her natural human nature is restored to its highest state. In the presence of Jesus' *being*, she has been redeemed from the degrading nature of lustful love to the selfless nature of sacred love. She has been reoriented toward her higher nature, and now she is on the mark. And Jesus affirms her transformation, saying, "Your faith has saved you; go in peace."

This is a line we hear over and over and over in the Jesus story: "Your faith has saved you." What is the nature of this faith? Faith is bestowed upon those people who have the capacity to recognize and awaken to divine *being*. Something about their state of suffering allows them to be open to his presence. The people who are in positions of power, who have money and authority in life—those people are frightened of Jesus. They eventually want him killed because he's an unsettling and unpredictable presence. That's the nature of spirit though; spirit *is* unpredictable. Through its very presence, it undermines hypocrisy and illusion. It's not tied to the domain of common ethics or the consensus reality of egoic consciousness. Spirit has its own morality, one that comes out of the direct knowing and connection of our shared unity.

So Mary recognizes Jesus and Jesus recognizes Mary. He peers through external appearances. He doesn't care who she's been, he doesn't care what she's done, he doesn't care how lost she might have been—all he cares about is the restoration of her *being*. When I read through this story, I find myself so very touched by her nature, which is to love much. Her nature is what led her to a life of lust and of selling herself for money. But that same nature in the presence of Jesus, in the presence of divine *being*, is what also saves her.

And I see this over again—that someone's greatest flaw ends up to be their greatest fortune, that through what is weakest within us, we find our strength. So it's not that Mary Magdalene has essentially changed. Her basic nature is her basic nature. Each human being is incarnated with certain qualities, with certain parts of their character set in stone, you might say. In fact, her character doesn't *need* to change; her problem isn't that she loves too much, but simply that, until she meets Jesus, she hadn't awakened to the higher dimension of love. So her innate capacity to love much is the key to her redemption. It is what is so beautiful about her character. All that she needed was to receive the redemptive grace of the radiance of *being*, embodied in Jesus.

Mary shows up in the Jesus story a number of times, but one of the most powerful moments occurs when she comes to the cross as Jesus is dying. She's one of three women there, holding vigil. She's also the first person to see Jesus when he's resurrected. So, though Mary isn't portrayed as one of the disciples, she in fact becomes a very close and intimate disciple. In my reading of the story, Mary is one of the most pivotal people in Jesus' life.

We pick up the story again when Mary comes to the tomb where Jesus is buried. When we were last exploring the crucifixion story, our perspective was informed by how the story appears in the Gospel of Mark; but now I'll pick up the story as it appears in the Gospel of John.

Mary stood weeping outside the tomb, and as she wept she stooped to look into the tomb. And she saw two angels in white, sitting where the body of Jesus had lain, one at the head and one at the feet. They said to her, "Woman, why are you weeping?" She said to them, "They have taken away my Lord, and I do not know where they have laid him." Having said this, she turned around and saw Jesus standing, but she did not know that it was Jesus. Jesus said to her, "Woman, why are you weeping? Whom are you seeking?" Supposing him to be the gardener, she said to him, "Sir, if you have carried him away, tell me where you have laid him, and I will take him away." Jesus said to her, "Mary." She turned and said to him in Aramaic, "Rabboni!" (which means *teacher*). Jesus said to her, "Do not cling to me, for I have not yet ascended to the Father; but go to my brothers and say to them, 'I am ascending to my Father and your Father, to my God and your God.'" Mary Magdalene went and announced to the disciples, "I have seen the Lord"—and that he had said these things to her. [John 20:11–18, ESV]

This is a beautiful moment, one of the most touching moments in the entire story. Mary is weeping at the tomb, and she looks in and sees two angels, who ask her why she's weeping. And when she first encounters Jesus she mistakes him for a gardener. She can't imagine that he would be there, alive, so she doesn't recognize him. He has to repeat again, "Mary"—and suddenly she recognizes him.

Mary has an instinctive way of knowing how to be in right relationship with divine *being* in the form of Jesus. As soon as she recognizes him, she says, "Teacher." She is instantaneously oriented in the correct way toward him. She doesn't see him as a friend, or as a parent, or as a lover—she sees him as what she knows him to be: teacher.

Maybe you can feel the deep simplicity in how she turns and says, "Teacher." There's such warmth there, such a beautiful and simple intimacy. And, as teacher, the next thing that Jesus says to her is, "Do not cling to me." This is his final teaching to her. This is his way of saying, "Don't try to hold on to me, don't desire me, but remember your true nature. Your nature is sacred love; your nature is divine *being*. Remember that, and you won't need to cling to me."

It's another intimate response by which he orients her one last little bit so that she doesn't cling. It's his final teaching to her. And that intimate moment of her reconnecting with him is almost like reconnecting with a beloved, or like reconnecting with God when you think God is gone. He's died, and yet now, there he is. They have this short but intense encounter in which he realigns her with her deeper nature. And in the end, her nature—to love much—is what saves her, through being reoriented toward its higher form of divine, non-clinging, selfless love.

Mary is a model not only of redemption—redemption through love, through the open heart, but also a model of devotion. At the moment when she recognizes Jesus as teacher, she has been reoriented and is in absolute devotion to him. She's in devotion to divine *being* at the end of Jesus' life, and she's in devotion to divine *being* at the very moment they met, when she spontaneously fell at his feet and wiped away her tears with her hair. This is a devotion that transcended otherness, a devotion that transcended her whole sense of herself, even the humiliation and shame that she felt at the moment of first encountering Jesus.

In reading the Gospels, you get the sense that Mary shows up at several important moments because, after she's encountered Jesus, she has an absolutely intimate knowledge of divine *being* unlike any of the other disciples. She gets it. She receives the liberating presence; she opens to the enlightening radiance. She knows what she is.

Mary is a reminder that it doesn't matter what you've done, it doesn't matter what you've gone through in life, it doesn't matter what you think about yourself, it doesn't matter what you *feel* about yourself. Everyone is redeemable. Everyone can turn around and hit the mark. Everyone can reorient toward divine *being*. No one need waste a moment in guilt about the past for Jesus didn't even imagine Mary as someone unredeemable. He immediately aligned with her state of openness and receptivity.

And now, here she is, she's weeping again because she can't find Jesus. He says to her, "Woman, why are you weeping?" And I love what he says next, "Whom are you seeking?" He knows whom she's seeking. Why would Jesus ask her this question? It's as if he's saying, "Mary, remember, there's nothing outside of yourself to seek. What are you doing? Whom are you seeking?" Otherwise there would be no reason for him to ask the question, because he already knows the answer. So again, his question offers her a subtle reminder, as if to say: it's all within you. The Kingdom of Heaven is within you; the redeeming presence is within you; you are infinitely more than you ever imagined yourself to be. What are you doing? Who are you looking for? It's all inside of *you*.

The life of Mary is a reminder that it doesn't matter what anyone's done. In the realm of divine *being*, nothing is important except the ability to recognize divinity when it shows up and respond to it with all your heart. In fact, the shame Mary first felt in the presence of Jesus may have made her available to recognize and respond to the divine presence when she came upon it. And so it is within most human beings' lives. We don't make the greatest leaps of consciousness when we're feeling great and everything is lovely and life is going our way. We often make the greatest leaps of consciousness through the moments of tragedy, through difficulty, through shame, through being stretched to the very limit. Why? Because that's when we're open and available. Our options have fallen away and, at the end of the day, there's really only two options left: simply to open yourself and surrender your holding or suffer.

Mary is a reminder of the ever-present power of redeeming grace. She's a mirror that shows us the model of true devotion. This is what the sacred heart looks like, how it responds, what it feels like inside—the closeness, the intimacy, the humility, the earthiness. These are the feminine qualities that she brings to the story, and they actually light up the whole story. Without Mary, the story wouldn't have anywhere near the same richness. Ultimately, she becomes a redeeming presence herself.

THE ARCHETYPE OF JOHN

The disciple John, called the beloved disciple, is a representative of someone who has an instinctive sense of how to be in the right relationship to Jesus. He is a metaphor for how to be in right relationship with the divine presence.

I want to begin the exploration of the character of John by reading the beginning of the Gospel of John. Now, almost all scholars agree that Jesus' disciple John is not the one who wrote the Gospel of John, but I think the theology in the Gospel of John actually hints at the disciple's real understanding of Jesus. As we look at this beloved follower, it's clear that he had the deepest understanding of Jesus among all the twelve disciples. John has a sense of ease, not only with Jesus but within himself. He's relaxed, at home in his own skin. And someone who is relaxed in his own humanity is much more likely to fall into right relationship with divine *being*.

The opening of the Gospel of John is among the best-known passages in the entire Bible, and some of the most beautiful poetry ever put to print.

In the beginning was the Word, and the Word was
with God, and the Word was God. He was in the
beginning with God. All things were made through
him, and without him was not any thing made that
was made. In him was life, and the life was the light
of men. The light shines in the darkness, and the
darkness has not overcome it.

There was a man sent from God, whose name was
John. He came as a witness, to bear witness about the
light, that all might believe through him. He was not
the light, but came to bear witness about the light.

The true light, which gives light to everyone, was
coming into the world. He was in the world, and the
world was made through him, yet the world did not
know him. He came to his own, and his own people
did not receive him. But to all who did receive him,
who believed in his name, he gave the right to become
children of God, who were born, not of blood nor of the
will of the flesh nor of the will of man, but of God.

And the Word became flesh and dwelt among us.
[John 1:1–14, ESV]

Now, that's a profound theology. John is saying that he sees
Jesus as being far beyond the form of his human incarnation;
he's recognized in Jesus the reality of divine *being*. Divine *being*
doesn't belong to anyone; it can't be possessed. Divine *being* is
the eternal word, the creative force in all of existence. So when
John sees Jesus, he doesn't get caught in the appearance of the
form, in the human appearance. John sees right into the ultimate reality that Jesus embodies.

Of course, someone with this instinct, with this deep spiritual understanding, would be at ease with himself. He would

not feel the need to struggle. It's no surprise that he'd be called the beloved follower, the one that Jesus loved most. He has an intimate friendship with Jesus. At the Last Supper, he's the one who leans against Jesus and who Jesus secretly whispers to about placing bread in the mouth of the one who will betray him.

John is the insider among the insiders. He is the archetype for our intuitive capacity to peer beyond the world of forms and touch the transcendent mystery at the center of our existence. If we're not caught in our ideas about ourselves, if we're not caught in the appearance of things, if our perception doesn't just stop at what our senses pick up, then we can sense this universal mystery. John is the archetype for someone who doesn't have to struggle for it, doesn't have to strive for it, doesn't have to go through great trials to find it—it's just part of his being.

Any spiritual seeker might think, "Wow, it would be absolutely wonderful to have it come that easily to me." But we must also remember that John had his human side. He also abandoned Jesus when Jesus was arrested. However, he did end up at the foot of the cross—the only male follower, and the only one of the twelve disciples who was there as Jesus died. And I think his presence there says something about John's character. He's always in the scene at the most important and intimate moments. He's close to the radiance; he watches and waits.

In a certain sense, John is also an archetype for that part of our *being* that watches, the divine witness untouched by what happens. The eternal witness within watches and waits, knowing that everything is well, that everything will unfold in its own way, in its own time. There's no rush, no hurry, and nothing that really needs to be done. So there's a sense of peace and well-being that comes from this watchful acceptance. That's the beloved disciple John's character; he watches and he waits, not caught up in all of the anxiety. He seems almost to hover above the story from beginning to end as a soothing presence. He doesn't always act perfectly—at times he gets frightened, at times he gets confused—but his deep underlying nature is of certainty and stillness. He is a man who is comfortable within himself.

We can look at ourselves through the lens of John as well. How do we see the world when we're in a state of ease, when we're not struggling, when we're not trying to attain or atone for anything? How do we see the world in those moments when we feel completely at peace in the universe, when quite out of nowhere we realize that everything is actually completely okay? In a sense, everything is divine from the very beginning. How, then, do we see the world?

All of the other gospel writers show Jesus experiencing trials and tribulations. In the Gospel of Mark, Jesus experiences real struggles and turmoil as he finds his role in life. Mark shows a very dynamic, human side of Jesus. In the Gospel of John, however, Jesus seems to hover above the human plane. John's Jesus feels more like a divine witness, never losing his equilibrium always in control of his emotions. John's Jesus has a certainty; he knows from the very beginning that no matter how bad it gets, everything is absolutely, totally okay and unfolding according to a divine plan.

The beloved disciple represents what it is to be at ease and comfortable within oneself. John has the nature of *agape*, of selfless love. He doesn't quarrel with people; he isn't self-serving; he is a devoted follower. Most human beings would love to be John, to meet someone like Jesus and respond the way he does. Yet within each being there is what John represents—that spark, that quiet little flicker of radiance that, when you touch upon it, you feel the perfection of the moment. You feel there's no rush and nothing that really needs to be accomplished. You might even start to touch upon the deeper understanding that everything is already divine as it is.

As Jesus said, "The Kingdom of Heaven is spread out upon the earth and men do not see it." [Gospel of Thomas 113] In other words, it's already done. Everything is already perfect, even amidst the chaos, amidst the ups and downs and the tragedies and the triumph. All this happens within the Kingdom, within the ultimate state of freedom. When we forget this, we become lost in the world of appearances and bound to the world of time with its worries and its doubts and its anxieties. But at any moment, we can turn to that still, small spark of eternity shining through the world of time that knows, always and eternally, that everything is somehow perfect within all of the chaos of life. The Kingdom of Heaven has already come and all you have to do is recognize it.

LIVING THE CHRIST 16

> There exists only the present instant . . .
> a Now which always and without end is itself new.
>
> MEISTER ECKHART

Today we're in need of a mythos that shows us what real, engaged spirituality looks like. The words of the Jesus story have inspired people for the better part of two thousand years. And yet, those words and images need us to breathe new life into them so that they once again come to life within us and reveal heaven here on earth. For Jesus the Christ walks amongst us even now, in the depths of our own consciousness, proclaiming the reality of eternal life that is present in the core of our *being*.

POURING OURSELVES INTO THE STORY

Until we pour ourselves into the story, until we become the story in ourselves, in our blood, flesh, and bones, it doesn't fully come alive. But when we give ourselves entirely to the Jesus story, we breathe the all-transforming spirit of new life and renew it. This is the only way that the story can come alive once again and reclaim the original power it once had before it became weighed down by centuries of egoic misunderstanding. When we *become* the story, we resurrect it from all of the old ways it has been presented to us by those who seek to control us more than to set us free, as Jesus had intended it to do.

Words are extraordinarily powerful. The words of the Jesus story have in many ways defined Western culture for two thousand years. But two thousand years is a long time for a story to survive, it's easy for the story to grow dusty and old and neglected. What I've tried to do in *Resurrecting Jesus*—and what I hope that I've accomplished in some small measure—is to invite *you* into the story, so that *you* make it your own.

There is no single correct interpretation of the Jesus story. It really doesn't matter whether we believe that every single scene is historically accurate or read the entire story as a myth or view it as something in between, a mixture of history and mythos. The important thing is not what we believe about the story, but whether we have the capacity to allow it to live within us, so that the story starts to speak to us in a way that's unique to us alone.

When we put ourselves in the place of all the different characters—whether it's in the place of Jesus, or one of the disciples, or one of the people who've been healed by Jesus, or even in the place of God—we start to see that contained within the story are many perspectives, many lenses to look through. When we look through the eyes of Jesus, the story looks one way; the story has a sense of vastness and purpose and vitality, a sense of eternity that Jesus embodies and that exists within us all. It's that spark of eternity that informs and brings life to the whole story. But we can also look at the story, as we've done in this book, through any of the disciples, each of whom offers their own lens, their own archetypal perspective.

Jesus, as always, represents the Christ. The Christ *is* that spark of eternity peering through the world of time and space. It transcends the mundane details of our life, but doesn't only transcend them; it actually has the power to breathe a new vitality into our lives so that spirit, the source of all vitality, is not disconnected from the ordinary moments of our lives. And each of the disciples shows a different way our humanity can relate to eternity. There are many ways that we as human beings can relate to our own divinity, to our search for that divinity, and to our discovery of that divinity within ourselves.

Contained within the Jesus story are the seeds of all these perspectives. My intention is to breathe a particular kind of spirit into this story—to bring forth Jesus the revolutionary, the radiant thread of divinity that breaks through old structures, that leaps beyond boundaries, that brings together and makes whole all the ways that our minds divide us from each other, even divide us within ourselves.

For me, one of the keys to deeply entering into the story, regardless of what interpretation you give it, is to sense how divinity—which you *are*—pours itself forth into incarnate life. *For God so loved the world, that he gave his only begotten son.*

Many of us are used to a kind of spirituality in which transcendence is emphasized almost exclusively, in which the way to deal with suffering and tragedy is to transcend our humanity, transcend the world of time and space. But the Jesus story shows us that there's a different way to look at our lives. There's a different spiritual movement, you might say, and it comes right at the beginning of the story when spirit descends into Jesus. That spirit—that's the Christ. Jesus is the human being who came to the River Jordan; Christ is the spirit that descended into him.

This is a different perspective, to have eternity *descending into* the world of time and space. It's not about getting out of the challenges of life, but about pouring oneself into life *as an act of redemptive love.* I think that this is one of the keys to really unlocking some of the mysteries of the Jesus story. It's an invitation to turn around the way that we have been taught to view life. We often see life as a vast universal experience that we're thrust into, and we're just little tiny individual human beings trying to relate to life and to each other, trying to find a way that life makes sense to us and helps us deal with the universal qualities of suffering and happiness and joy and sorrow.

The message of the Jesus story is that we must fully enter the world—and that the way to freedom is through pouring ourselves into life, through saying yes in the biggest, boldest, possible way. And we can only do that when we connect with that sense of well-being, which is love. Love doesn't ultimately concern itself with questions like, "Am I having a great time?" It doesn't concern itself with the ego's search to have a better and better experience. Love is a completely different energy. Love pours itself forth, gives itself fully; love finds its fulfillment by offering itself. I've always been struck by how the Jesus story conveys this sense of lavishly opening oneself to life as a means of discovering the radiance of eternity.

The story reflects back to us our divinity. Jesus is a metaphor, a symbol for the divinity that exists within us all, the timelessness of eternity peering through the world of time. When we see Jesus this way, the whole Jesus story begins to come alive, because then we have not separated ourselves from the vitality source, from divine *being* itself. Heaven and earth are brought together where they have always belonged, and we can then embody our true potential to pour forth the redeeming presence of divine love into every aspect of our lives.

But the story isn't *only* about looking at our lives through the eyes of eternity, through the eyes of Jesus the Christ. It's also about a deep and profound humanity, about coming to grips with the frail and imperfect parts of human nature. And this is where the disciples come in: they are all different perspectives on our humanity. There is part of us that is drawn to the light of *being,* but also frightened of it. There is part of us that has a great confidence in what we're capable of, but sometimes overestimates our capacity. There is part of us that has a deep belief in our essential unworthiness, an essential sense of lack that doesn't allow us to fully open to the Christ's presence. Each of the disciples shows a different way that our humanity relates to our divinity, and I think this is an extraordinarily important thing to understand about the Jesus story.

I think the story comes fully alive when we look at our own human lives, with all their ups and downs, through the eyes of Christ, through the eyes of eternal *being.* We are the essential vitality source; it's not out there; it's not other than us. We are the ones who have the capacity to breathe new life into the Jesus story and, in doing so, we can also breathe new life into our own human stories—because each of us is a story. Essentially, we are eternal *being,* but each of us lives a human drama, the moment-to-moment unfolding of our lives. This is the challenge of the Jesus story. Are we willing to really consent to our own lives, to pour ourselves forth, to give ourselves entirely to our own human experience?

THE PRESENCE OF UNIVERSAL LOVE

When the eternal and the human meet, *that's* where love is born. That's where *agape,* selfless love, bursts forth—not through escaping our humanity or trying to disappear into transcendence, but through finding that place where they come into union. That's what breathes a new spirit into our lives and opens us to the presence of the Christian message.

I imagine everyone has had the experience of walking into an old church and immediately being struck by that quality of presence, that particular energetic signature that we associate with Christianity. That energetic signature of the Christ presence—or the Christ transmission, as we would say in Zen—is something that many of us are familiar with. That signature is one of a deep love and a transcendent well-being that we sense is also, strangely, here and now and present. This is the other face of Jesus—the Jesus of great love and great compassion, the Jesus that cared so much that he completely gave himself to life in order to redeem it.

When we encounter the Christ presence, it reminds us that there's something deep within ourselves that is unfathomable, mysterious, and absolutely, unreservedly loving. I think that most people who've experienced the Christian message deeply have felt this energetic vibration of Christianity. We don't need to see ourselves as Christians to partake of the Christ essence, because it's a universal energy, a universal gift that we can all receive.

This is a particular way of experiencing the Jesus story, experiencing the reality of the Christ presence, and it's one that's familiar to us even in the churches. Of course, it's also a way of *interpreting* the story. There is Jesus the lover of humanity; Jesus the man of exquisite compassion, giving himself into humanity to redeem it; and Jesus as the Christ presence who helps reorient us to what is eternal and divine in us when we have missed the mark. Some version of this view, I think, is what we likely associate with Christianity and the Christian message.

Through this book, I hope to bring forth part of the Christian story that has been lost to some extent—that sense of Jesus as a vital spiritual revolutionary. This Jesus comes not so much to comfort us as to confront us. This Jesus is the energy of eternity fully embodying itself, breaking through all the false boundaries and imaginary dividing lines that separate us as human beings and separate us from the world. And once all those boundaries are broken, we can all come together, because what separates us is just an idea. Even the feeling that the Christ essence is something *out there*, something far away, is just an idea. And I can imagine Christ trying to destroy that boundary as well; as he himself said, "The Kingdom of God is spread upon the earth, and men do not see it."

The Kingdom isn't far away. The Kingdom is right here and right now. The challenge of Jesus' message is that it constantly asks of us: Can you see it? Can you see the kingdom right now? Right in the midst of this very moment, in the midst of this very life that often seems mundane and ordinary—can you see eternity? Have you allowed your self and your world to be rendered transparent to the underlying divinity that shines through it?

This teaching is as true and vital and necessary now as it ever was. But in order to express the perennial truths and realities of the Jesus story, it seems to me that we need a new mythos, one that can show us what embodied spirit really looks like and how sacred love moves in the world of time and space. When we embody this mythos, then this engaged and embodied spirituality starts to come alive within us—not as an idea, not as a belief, not as an ideal that we're trying to conform to, but as our own unique expression of divinity.

Each of us must discover for ourselves what the Jesus story means. What does this story mean to *you?* What challenges does it present you with? What does it remind you of that you may have forgotten? What does it bring forth in you? What does it tell you that you need to pay attention to, to give yourself to, to pour yourself forth into? How does it reflect any ways that you may be holding back, holding on, letting fear dominate your life?

There is a wonderful quote from the Gospel of Thomas in which Jesus says, "Anyone living from the living will not die." This is a challenge of the Jesus story—to live from the living of our own lives. What would that mean for you if you were to live from the living of your own life, if you were to live from that vitality source that peers through your whole existence? What kind of boundary lines and false separations does this story ask you to go beyond? How might your life be different if you really embodied the spirit of love pouring itself into the world of time and space? How might it be different if you embodied the revolutionary spirit that moves boldly and fearlessly through life and always lives within the question of truth, the central question of our lives?

Pontius Pilate asked Jesus, "What is truth?" We ask ourselves, what's the truth of my life? What do I need to do to bring forth that light in *my* life, into the entirety of my human existence? There's another quote from the Gospel of Thomas that reads, "There is light within a man of light and he lights up the whole world. If he does not shine, he is darkness." [Gospel of Thomas 24] This presents a challenge to each one of us. Within each one of us *is* the divine light; the challenge is to bring it forth—not to keep it hidden, or dimmed down out of fear, but to open ourselves so that that transcendence, that infinity, can experience itself fully as this human incarnation.

As Christ said, if we don't do this, we will live in darkness. We will have fallen asleep to our own light, to our own life. As the Jesus story shows us, when we live from our own light, from the deepest sense of vitality within us, life does not necessarily always feel secure. It requires courage and openness to constantly lean in to the cutting edge, to what really feels true and real.

Ultimately, what allows us to embody the full measure of our life is a sense of stillness. One of the underlying, almost unspoken themes of the Jesus story is the stillness of eternity. It's Jesus in the desert, Jesus on top of the mountain. In such moments of aloneness, we give ourselves to that which is quiet within, to the deepest type of listening. True spiritual action in the world comes from a deep sense of inner stillness, rooted in that point around which the changing world revolves. And within the changing world is that spark of eternity—always free, always content, always the quiet and silent life-giver to our lives.

ACKNOWLEDGMENTS

This book is a product of the love and dedication of many people. I offer a deep bow of appreciation to Mitchell Clute. Your enthusiastic support of this project and fine editing skills were a true gift. Every time we talked, I left with a smile on my face. I also offer my deepest gratitude to Tami Simon. Your unwavering integrity, curiosity, and dedication to truth are always a breath of fresh air, and your friendship is one of the great gifts of this life.

I also want to acknowledge some of the Christian writers who have been the most inspirational to me over the years: Meister Eckhart, one of the true giants in the history of Christian mysticism, for his brilliant and enlightened sermons on the mystery of Christ. Saint John of the Cross, for his great insights into the mystical journey and his lyrical poetry. Thomas Merton, for first opening my eyes to the deeper meaning of the Christian journey. Joseph Campbell, for his great insights into the mythic understanding of the world's great stories. John Carroll, for showing me the significance of the Gospel of Mark and for some of the most powerful writing I have ever encountered.

ABOUT THE AUTHOR

Adyashanti (whose name means "primordial peace") dares all seekers of peace and freedom to take the possibility of liberation in this life seriously. He began teaching in 1996 at the request of his Zen teacher with whom he had been studying for fourteen years. Since then, many spiritual seekers have awakened to their true nature while spending time with Adyashanti.

The author of *Falling Into Grace, Emptiness Dancing, The Impact of Awakening, True Meditation, The End of Your World,* and *My Secret Is Silence,* Adyashanti offers spontaneous and direct nondual teachings that have been compared to those of the early Zen masters and Advaita Vedanta sages. However, Adya says, "If you filter my words through any tradition or '-ism,' you will miss altogether what I am saying. The liberating truth is not static; it is alive. It cannot be put into concepts and be understood by the mind. The truth lies beyond all forms of conceptual fundamentalism. What you are is the beyond—awake and present, here and now already. I am simply helping you to realize that."

A native of northern California, Adyashanti lives with his wife, Annie (Mukti), and teaches extensively in the San Francisco Bay Area, offering *satsangs,* weekend intensives, and silent retreats. He also travels to teach in other areas of the United States and Canada. For more information, please visit adyashanti.org.

ABOUT SOUNDS TRUE

Sounds True is a multimedia publisher whose mission is to inspire and support personal transformation and spiritual awakening. Founded in 1985 and located in Boulder, Colorado, we work with many of the leading spiritual teachers, thinkers, healers, and visionary artists of our time. We strive with every title to preserve the essential "living wisdom" of the author or artist. It is our goal to create products that not only provide information to a reader or listener, but that also embody the quality of a wisdom transmission.

For those seeking genuine transformation, Sounds True is your trusted partner. At SoundsTrue.com you will find a wealth of free resources to support your journey, including exclusive weekly audio interviews, free downloads, interactive learning tools, and other special savings on all our titles.

To learn more, please visit SoundsTrue.com/bonus/free_gifts or call us toll free at 800-333-9185.

SOUNDS TRUE
many voices, one journey